Collins

INTERNATIONAL PRIMARY SCIENCE

Teacher's Guide 1

William Collins' dream of knowledge for all began with the publication of his first book in 1819. A self-educated mill worker, he not only enriched millions of lives, but also founded a flourishing publishing house. Today, staying true to this spirit, Collins books are packed with inspiration, innovation and practical expertise. They place you at the centre of a world of possibility and give you exactly what you need to explore it.

Collins. Freedom to teach.

Published by Collins
An imprint of HarperCollins*Publishers* Ltd.
The News Building
1 London Bridge Street
London
SE1 9GF

Browse the complete Collins catalogue at
www.collins.co.uk

© HarperCollins*Publishers* Limited 2014

10 9 8

ISBN: 978-0-00-758610-3

The authors assert their moral rights to be identified as the authors of this work.

Contributing authors: Phillipa Skillicorn, Karen Morrison, Tracey Baxter, Sunetra Berry, Pat Dower, Helen Harden, Pauline Hannigan, Anita Loughrey, Emily Miller, Jonathan Miller, Anne Pilling, Pete Robinson.

The exam-style questions and sample answers used in the Assessment Sheets have been written by the author.

British Library Cataloguing in Publication Data
A Catalogue record for this publication is available from the British Library.

Commissioned by Elizabeth Catford
Project managed by Karen Williams
Series editor: Karen Morrison
Design and production by Ken Vail Graphic Design

Acknowledgements
The publishers wish to thank the following for permission to reproduce photographs.
Every effort has been made to trace copyright holders and to obtain their permission for the use of copyright materials. The publishers will gladly receive any information enabling them to rectify any error or omission at the first opportunity.
COVER: Volodymyr Burdiak / Shutterstock.com

Contents

Introduction

About *Collins International Primary Science*

Collins International Primary Science is specifically written to fully meet the requirements of the Cambridge Primary Science curriculum framework from Cambridge Assessment International Education and the material has been carefully developed to meet the needs of primary science students and teachers in a range of international contexts.

Content is organised according to the three main strands: Biology, Chemistry and Physics and the skills detailed under the Scientific Enquiry strand are introduced and taught in the context of those areas.

All course materials make use of the fully-integrated digital resources available on the DVD. For example, video clips and slideshows allow students the opportunity to view at first-hand examples of habitats, plants and animals they may not be familiar with from their own country. The interactive activities provide a valuable teaching resource that will engage the students and consolidate learning.

Components of the course

For each of Stages 1 to 6 as detailed in the Cambridge Primary Science Framework, we offer:

- A full colour, highly illustrated and photograph rich Student's Book
- A write-in Workbook linked to the Student's Book
- This comprehensive Teacher's Guide with clear suggestions for using the materials, including the electronic components of the course
- A DVD which contains slideshows, video clips, additional photographs and interactive activities for use in the classroom.

Approach

The course is designed with student-centred learning at its heart. The students conduct investigations with guidance and support from their teacher. Their investigations respond to questions asked by the teacher or asked by the students themselves. They are practical and activity-based, and include observing,

questioning, making and testing predictions, collecting and recording simple data, observing patterns and suggesting explanations. Plenty of opportunity is provided for the students to consolidate and apply what they have learned and to relate what they are doing in science to other curriculum areas and the environment in which they live.

Much of the students' work is conducted as paired work or in small groups, in line with international best practice. Activities are designed to be engaging for students and to support teachers in their assessment of student progress and achievement. Each lesson is planned to support clear learning objectives and outcomes, to provide students and teachers with a good view of the learning. The activities within each unit provide opportunities for oral and written feedback by the teacher, peer teaching and peer assessment within small groups.

Throughout the course, there is wide variety of learning experiences on offer. The materials are structured so that they do not impose a rigid structure but rather provide a range of options linked to the learning objectives. Teachers are able to select from these to provide an interesting, exciting and appropriate learning experience that is suited to their particular classroom situations.

Differentiation

Differentiation is clearly built into the lesson plans in this Teacher's Guide and levels are indicated against the Student's Book activities. You will see that the practical activities offer three levels of differentiated demand. The square activities are appropriate for the level of nearly all of the students. The circle questions are appropriate for the level of most of the students (this is the level students should be achieving for this stage). The triangle questions are appropriate for some students of higher ability. Teachers may find that achievement levels vary for different content strands and interest levels. So students who are working at the circle level in Biology may find Chemistry or Physics topics more interesting and/or easier, so they may work at a different level for some of the time.

Teacher's Guide

Each double-page spread covers one unit in the Student's Book. Each unit has a clear structure identified by the *Introduction–Teaching and learning activities–Consolidate and review* sequence.

Safety notes and any other useful notes for the teacher appear here.

Scientific enquiry skills from Cambridge Primary curriculum covered in the unit are provided as a useful reference for the teacher.

The main **learning objectives** for this unit.

Resources the teacher will require for this unit.

Classroom equipment the teacher will require for this unit.

Key words are repeated from the Student's Book page for the teacher to reinforce during the unit.

Scientific background – a brief summary of the science background that the teacher may find useful for this unit.

Introduction – this is the introductory part of the unit where ideas are beginning to be explored and students reflect on prior learning and share objectives.

Teaching and learning activities – this leads into the main lesson.

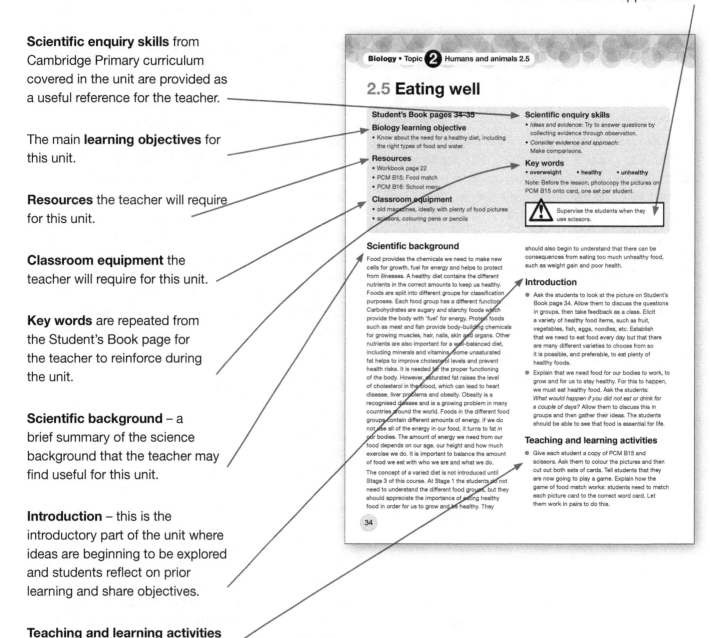

Biology • Topic **2** Humans and animals 2.5

2.5 Eating well

Student's Book pages 34–35

Biology learning objective
• Know about the need for a healthy diet, including the right types of food and water.

Resources
• Workbook page 22
• PCM B15: Food match
• PCM B16: School menu

Classroom equipment
• old magazines, ideally with plenty of food pictures
• scissors, colouring pens or pencils

Scientific enquiry skills
• *Ideas and evidence:* Try to answer questions by collecting evidence through observation.
• *Consider evidence and approach:* Make comparisons.

Key words
• overweight   • healthy   • unhealthy

Note: Before the lesson, photocopy the pictures on PCM B15 onto card, one set per student.

⚠ Supervise the students when they use scissors.

Scientific background

Food provides the chemicals we need to make new cells for growth, fuel for energy and helps to protect from illnesses. A healthy diet contains the different nutrients in the correct amounts to keep us healthy. Foods are split into different groups for classification purposes. Each food group has a different function. Carbohydrates are sugary and starchy foods which provide the body with 'fuel' for energy. Protein foods such as meat and fish provide body-building chemicals for growing muscles, hair, nails, skin and organs. Other nutrients are also important for a well-balanced diet, including minerals and vitamins. Some unsaturated fat helps to improve cholesterol levels and prevent health risks. It is needed for the proper functioning of the body. However, saturated fat raises the level of cholesterol in the blood, which can lead to heart disease, liver problems and obesity. Obesity is a recognised disease and is a growing problem in many countries around the world. Foods in the different food groups contain different amounts of energy. If we do not use all of the energy in our food, it turns to fat in our bodies. The amount of energy we need from our food depends on our age, our height and how much exercise we do. It is important to balance the amount of food we eat with who we are and what we do.

The concept of a varied diet is not introduced until Stage 3 of this course. At Stage 1 the students do not need to understand the different food groups, but they should appreciate the importance of eating healthy food in order for us to grow and be healthy. They

should also begin to understand that there can be consequences from eating too much unhealthy food, such as weight gain and poor health.

Introduction

● Ask the students to look at the picture on Student's Book page 34. Allow them to discuss the questions in groups, then take feedback as a class. Elicit a variety of healthy food items, such as fruit, vegetables, fish, eggs, noodles, etc. Establish that we need to eat food every day but that there are many different varieties to choose from so it is possible, and preferable, to eat plenty of healthy foods.

● Explain that we need food for our bodies to work, to grow and for us to stay healthy. For this to happen, we must eat healthy food. Ask the students: *What would happen if you did not eat or drink for a couple of days?* Allow them to discuss this in groups and then gather their ideas. The students should be able to see that food is essential for life.

Teaching and learning activities

● Give each student a copy of PCM B15 and scissors. Ask them to colour the pictures and then cut out both sets of cards. Tell students that they are now going to play a game. Explain how the game of food match works: students need to match each picture card to the correct word card. Let them work in pairs to do this.

34

Graded activities – these are differentiated to suit three different levels of ability. They will often involve an investigation and practical element.

The **Consolidate and review** section is used to reinforce the students' learning during the lesson.

Differentiation – this section discusses the differentiated learning outcomes and provides the teacher with an idea of the likely behaviours of students of different ability, referencing the square, circle and triangle icons which are used across the course.

Links to the **Collins Big Cat** reading scheme are provided to relate science activities to the English that the students are learning.

Biology • Topic ② Humans and animals 2.5

- Ask the students to sort the food picture cards from PCM B15 into groups according to their own criteria. Some students may sort the foods into those that they like and those that they do not. Others will begin to think of them in terms of how healthy they are or in basic food groups. Discuss with the students why they have grouped their foods in a certain way. This is a good opportunity to recap foods from other cultures.
- Remind students that we only need to eat certain types of foods in small amounts. Ask: *Why should we not eat too much sugary food? Why should we not eat too much fatty food?* Take suggestions from the class. Explain that we can become overweight and unhealthy.
- Ask the students to look at the pictures on Student's Book page 35. Allow them to discuss the questions in groups, then take feedback as a class.

Graded activities

1 Give each pair of students some old magazines and scissors. Ask them to cut out as many pictures of different foods as they can and then to sort the pictures into two groups: *healthy* and *unhealthy*. The pictures may be of single food items, several combined together, e.g. a sandwich, or complete meals. Once the sorting is done, ask the students to give reasons for why they have sorted the foods into each category. Ask: *Was it difficult to decide which group to put some of the food in?* This could lead to a discussion about some meals containing a mixture of healthy and unhealthy foods.

2 Ask the students to think about their favourite healthy meal and to draw a picture of it on Workbook page 22. They should then label the picture, in their own language or in English. Depending on ability, some students may add one label for the complete meal or more able students may label the individual food items. When they have completed their drawings, let the students discuss the favourite healthy meals in groups. Take feedback as a class and establish the most popular healthy meals. Stress the importance of fruit and vegetables, foods such as rice, pasta and potatoes (carbohydrates), milk and cheese (dairy), and fish and meat (proteins). (At this stage, students do not need to know the food categories shown in parentheses, only examples of healthy foods.)

3 Ask the students to name some different healthy foods. They should think of individual foods, such as meat, fish, bread, carrots, etc. rather than complete meals or food groups, e.g. vegetables. Compile a class list on the board. Elicit as wide a variety of food items as possible. Once you have created an extensive list, give each student a copy of PCM B16. Tell the students that they need to work in groups to design a healthy menu for a week at school. They can use the list on the board to give them ideas and add any others that they can think of. Once they have completed their menus, invite each group to present their menu to the class. You could then take a class vote on the best overall menu or best individual days.

Consolidate and review

- Tell students to pretend that they are going to live on a desert island for a week. There is no food on the island and no shops. They need to take everything they need with them. In groups, the students should decide what food and drink they would like to take.

Differentiation

■ All of the students should be able to identify the healthy and unhealthy foods and correctly sort them into two groups. Circulate and explain any of the food items which may be unfamiliar to the students.

● Most of the students should be able to draw an accurate picture of their chosen meal and add labels with little help, either labelling the meal as a whole or the individual elements.

▲ Some of the students should be able to work together to share ideas and think critically to design a menu which incorporates a range of healthy foods. Some may struggle to create a number of different meals. If so, remind them to look at the class list on the board and make suggestions for how different foods can be combined to make a meal. Ask questions to guide their thinking.

Big Cat
Students who read *Big Cat We like fruit* will recognise the different types of fruit shown in this book.

35

At the end of each Topic the answers to the Student's Book questions and Assessment Sheets are given in full.

At the back of this Teacher's Guide are the Photocopy Masters (PCMs) and Assessment Sheets. These can be photocopied and handed out to the students as necessary.

Student's Book

Each double page spread covers one unit. Each page has photographs or graphics to provide a stimulus for discussions and questions.

Key words – these are the words that the students will learn and use for this unit.

Questions – These can be used as whole class discussion points and also to enable the teacher to assess how well individual students understand the unit.

Activities

1. Square questions are appropriate for the level of nearly all of the students.

2. Circle questions are appropriate for the level of most of the students (this is the level students should be achieving for this stage).

3. Triangle questions are appropriate for some students of higher ability.

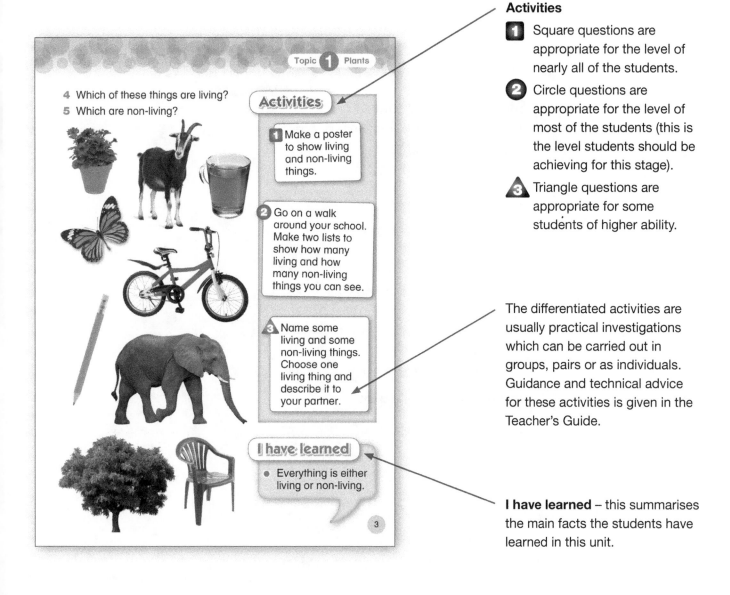

The differentiated activities are usually practical investigations which can be carried out in groups, pairs or as individuals. Guidance and technical advice for these activities is given in the Teacher's Guide.

I have learned – this summarises the main facts the students have learned in this unit.

At the back of the Student's Book is a comprehensive **Glossary** of all the Key words that are used during the lessons.

Workbook

The Workbook is for students to record observations, investigation results and key learning during the lesson. It has structured spaces for the students to record work and guidance on what to do. It gives the teacher an opportunity to give the student written feedback and becomes part of each student's work portfolio.

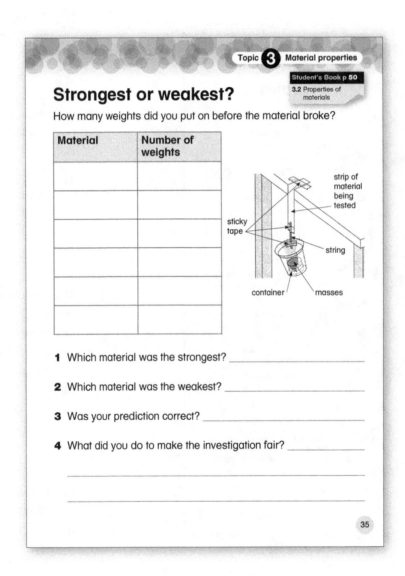

Strongest or weakest?

Student's Book p **50**
3.2 Properties of materials

How many weights did you put on before the material broke?

Material	Number of weights

strip of material being tested

sticky tape

string

container   masses

1 Which material was the strongest? _____

2 Which material was the weakest? _____

3 Was your prediction correct? _____

4 What did you do to make the investigation fair? _____

_____

_____

35

DVD

The DVD provides teachers with a set of electronic resources to support learning and assessment. The lesson plans in this Teacher's Guide give references in the *Resources* box and in the body of text to the relevant video clips, slideshows and interactive 'drag and drop' activities.

Interactive 'drag and drop' activities

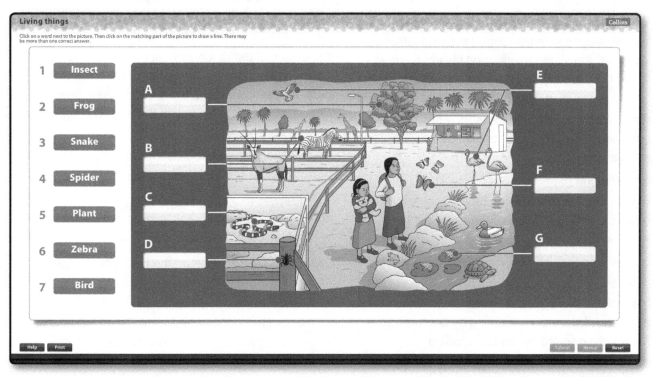

Slideshows and video clips

Assessment in primary science

In the primary science programme, assessment is a continuous, planned process that involves collecting information about student progress and learning in order to provide constructive feedback to students and parents, but also to inform planning and the next teaching steps.

Cambridge Assessment International Education Primary curriculum framework for science makes it clear what the students are expected to learn and achieve at each level. Our task as teachers is to make sure that we assess whether (or not) the students have achieved the stated goals using clearly-focused, varied, reliable and flexible methods of assessment.

In the Collins Primary Science course, assessment is continuous and in-built. It applies the principles of international best practice and ensures that assessment:

● is ongoing and regular

● supports individual achievement and allows for the students to reflect on their learning and set targets for themselves

● provides feedback and encouragement to the students

● allows for the integration of assessment into activities and classroom teaching by combining different assessment methods, including observations, questioning, self-assessment, formal and informal tasks

● uses strategies that cater for the variety of student needs in the classroom (language, physical, emotional and cultural), and acknowledges that the students do not all need to be assessed at the same time or in the same way

● allows for more formal summative assessment including controlled activities, tasks and class tests.

Assessing scientific enquiry skills

The development of scientific enquiry skills needs to be monitored. You need to check that the students acquire the basic skills as you teach and make sure that they are able to apply them in more complex activities and situations later on.

You can do this by identifying the assessment opportunities in different enquiry-based tasks and by asking appropriate informal assessment questions as the students work through and complete the tasks.

For example, the students may be involved in an activity where they are expected to plan and carry out a fair test investigating cars and ramps (*Plan investigative work: Recognise that a test or comparison may be unfair*).

As the students work through the activity you have the opportunity to assess whether they are able to identify:

● one thing that will change

● what things they will measure and record

● what things will be kept the same.

Once they have completed the task, you can ask some informal assessment questions, such as:

● Is a test the only way to do a scientific investigation? (*No, there are other methods of collecting and recording information, including using secondary sources.*)

● Is every test a fair test?

● Are there special things we need to do to make sure a test is fair?

● What should we do before we can carry out a fair test properly? (*Develop and write up a plan.*)

● Is a fair test in science the same as a written science or maths test at school?

● How is it different?

Formal written assessment

The Collins Primary Science course offers a selection of Assessment Sheets that teachers can use to formally assess learning and to award marks if necessary. These sheets include questions posed in different ways, questions where the students fill in answers or draw diagrams and true or false questions among others.

Below are some examples of the types of questions, provided on the Assessment Sheets. The Assessment Sheets can be found at the back of this Teacher's Guide.

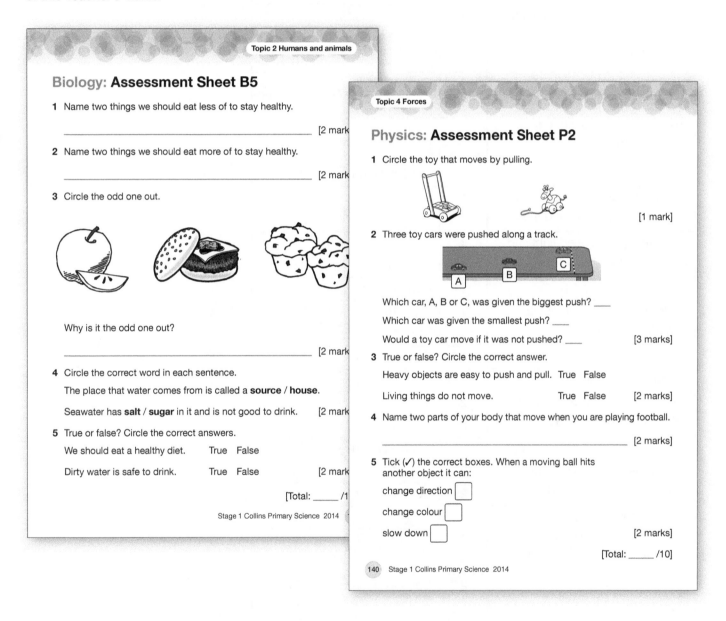

Topic 2 Humans and animals

Biology: Assessment Sheet B5

1 Name two things we should eat less of to stay healthy.

_____ [2 mark

2 Name two things we should eat more of to stay healthy.

_____ [2 mark

3 Circle the odd one out.

Why is it the odd one out?

_____ [2 mark

4 Circle the correct word in each sentence.

The place that water comes from is called a **source / house**.

Seawater has **salt / sugar** in it and is not good to drink. [2 mark

5 True or false? Circle the correct answers.

We should eat a healthy diet.   True   False

Dirty water is safe to drink.   True   False   [2 mark

[Total: _____ /1

Stage 1 Collins Primary Science 2014

Topic 4 Forces

Physics: Assessment Sheet P2

1 Circle the toy that moves by pulling.

[1 mark]

2 Three toy cars were pushed along a track.

Which car, A, B or C, was given the biggest push? ____

Which car was given the smallest push? ____

Would a toy car move if it was not pushed? ____   [3 marks]

3 True or false? Circle the correct answer.

Heavy objects are easy to push and pull.   True   False

Living things do not move.   True   False   [2 marks]

4 Name two parts of your body that move when you are playing football.

_____ [2 marks]

5 Tick (✓) the correct boxes. When a moving ball hits another object it can:

change direction ☐

change colour ☐

slow down ☐   [2 marks]

[Total: _____ /10]

140   Stage 1 Collins Primary Science 2014

In addition to the materials supplied in the course, schools may opt for their students to take standardised Cambridge Assessment International Education progression tests at Stages 3, 4, 5 and 6. These tests are developed by Cambridge but they are written and marked in schools. Teachers download the tests and administer them in their own classrooms. Cambridge Assessment International Education provides a mark scheme and you can upload learners' test results and then analyse the results and create and print reports. You can also compare a learner's results against their class, school or other schools around the world and on a year-by-year basis.

Learning objectives matching grid

Stage 1 Biology Learning Objectives	Topic	Unit	Teacher's Guide pages
Plants			
Know that plants are living things.	1	2	4
	1	3	6
	1	Consolidation	24
Know that there are living things and things that have never been alive.	1	1	2
	1	2	4
	1	4	8
	1	Consolidation	24
Explore ways that different animals and plants inhabit local environments.	1	5	10
	1	6	12
	1	7	14
	1	Consolidation	24
Name the major parts of a plant, looking at real plants and models.	1	8	16
	1	12	24
Know that plants need light and water to grow.	1	3	6
	1	9	18
	1	Consolidation	24
Explore how seeds grow into flowering plants.	1	10	20
	1	11	22
	1	Consolidation	24
Humans and animals			
Recognise the similarities and differences between each other.	2	1	26
	2	2	28
	2	Consolidation	46
Recognise and name the main external parts of the body.	2	3	30
	2	Consolidation	46
Know about the need for a healthy diet, including the right types of food and water.	2	4	32
	2	5	34
	2	6	36
	2	Consolidation	46
Explore how senses enable humans and animals to be aware of the world around them.	2	7	38
	2	8	40
	2	9	42
	2	Consolidation	46
Know that humans and animals produce offspring which grow into adults.	2	10	44
	2	Consolidation	46

Stage 1 Chemistry Learning Objectives	Topic	Unit	Teacher's Guide pages
Material properties			
Use senses to explore and talk about different materials.	3	1	48
	3	Consolidation	62
Identify the characteristics of different materials.	3	2	50
	3	3	52
	3	Consolidation	62
Recognise and name common materials.	3	4	54
	3	5	56
	3	Consolidation	62
Sort objects into groups based on the properties of their materials.	3	6	58
	3	7	60
	3	Consolidation	62

Stage 1 Physics Learning Objectives	Topic	Unit	Teacher's Guide pages
Forces			
Explore, talk about and describe the movement of familiar things.	4	1	64
	4	Consolidation	74
Recognise that both pushes and pulls are forces.	4	2	66
	4	3	68
	4	Consolidation	74
Recognise that when things speed up, slow down or change direction there is a cause.	4	4	70
	4	5	72
	4	Consolidation	74
Sound			
Identify many sources of sound.	5	1	76
	5	2	78
	5	4	82
	5	Consolidation	88
Know that we hear when sound enters our ear.	5	3	80
	5	4	82
	5	5	84
	5	Consolidation	88
Recognise that as sound travels from a source it becomes fainter.	5	5	84
	5	6	86
	5	Consolidation	88

Scientific enquiry skills matching grid

Stage 1 Scientific enquiry skills	Topic	Unit	Teacher's Guide page
Ideas and evidence			
Try to answer questions by collecting evidence through observation.	1	1	2
	1	2	4
	1	4	8
	1	5	10
	1	6	12
	1	10	20
	1	11	22
	2	1	26
	2	3	30
	2	4	32
	2	5	34
	2	7	38
	2	8	40
	2	9	42
	2	10	44
	3	1	48
	3	2	50
	3	3	52
	3	4	54
	3	6	58
	3	7	60
	4	1	64
	4	1	66
	4	4	70
	4	5	72
	5	1	76
	5	2	78
	5	3	80
	5	4	82
	5	5	84
	5	6	86

Stage 1 Scientific enquiry skills	Topic	Unit	Teacher's Guide page
Plan investigative work			
Ask questions and contribute to discussions about how to seek answers.	1	5	10
	1	7	14
	1	9	18
	2	6	36
	2	10	44
	3	2	50
	4	3	68
	4	4	70
	4	5	72
	5	4	82
	5	5	84
	5	6	86
Make predictions.	1	3	6
	1	5	10
	1	7	14
	1	9	18
	1	10	20
	2	2	28
	2	6	36
	3	2	50
	3	3	52
	3	7	60
	4	3	68
	4	4	70
	4	5	72
	5	2	78
	5	3	80
	5	4	82
	5	5	84
	5	6	86
Decide what to do to try to answer a science question.	1	7	14
	1	9	18
	3	5	56
	3	7	60
	4	3	68
	4	4	70
	4	5	72
	5	4	82
	5	5	84
	5	6	86

Stage 1 Scientific enquiry skills	Topic	Unit	Teacher's Guide page
Obtain and present evidence			
Explore and observe in order to collect evidence (measurements and observations) to answer questions.	1	3	6
	1	7	14
	1	8	16
	1	9	18
	1	10	20
	2	2	28
	2	6	36
	3	2	50
	3	3	52
	3	7	60
	4	3	68
	4	4	70
	4	5	72
	5	2	78
	5	3	80
	5	4	82
	5	5	84
	5	6	86
Suggest ideas and follow instructions.	1	9	18
	3	2	50
	3	3	52
	3	5	56
	4	3	68
	4	4	70
	4	5	72
	5	4	82
	5	5	84
	5	6	86
Record stages in work.	1	7	14
	1	9	18
	1	10	20
	3	2	50
	3	3	52
	3	7	60
	4	3	68
	4	4	70
	4	5	72
	5	4	82
	5	5	84
	5	6	86

Stage 1 Scientific enquiry skills	Topic	Unit	Teacher's Guide page
Consider evidence and approach			
Make comparisons.	1	2	4
	1	4	8
	1	5	10
	2	2	28
	2	5	34
	2	10	44
	3	2	50
	3	3	52
	3	7	60
	4	3	68
	4	4	70
	4	5	72
	5	2	78
	5	5	84
	5	6	86
Compare what happened with predictions.	1	3	6
	1	5	10
	1	7	14
	1	9	18
	1	10	20
	2	2	28
	2	6	36
	3	2	50
	3	3	52
	3	7	60
	4	3	68
	4	4	70
	4	5	72
	5	2	78
	5	3	80
	5	4	82
	5	5	84
	5	6	86
Model and communicate ideas in order to share, explain and develop them.	1	7	14
	1	8	16
	2	4	32
	3	5	56
	5	5	84
	5	6	86

Lesson plans

1.1 Is it alive?

Student's Book pages 2–3
Biology learning objective
- Know that there are living things and things that have never been alive.

Resources
- Workbook page 1
- Slideshow B1: Is it living or non-living?
- PCM B1: Living or non-living?

Classroom equipment
- large sheets of paper
- coloured pens or pencils
- scissors
- glue
- selection of old magazines
- a doll

Scientific enquiry skills
- *Ideas and evidence:* Try to answer questions by collecting evidence through observation.

Key words
- **living**
- **non-living**

⚠ Supervise the students when they use scissors. If you take the students on a walk around the school grounds, ensure they are safe and that they stay together. They should not put anything they find into their mouths.

Scientific background

Everything in the world can be sorted into *living* or *non-living*. In Unit 1.2, the students will learn that if something is living it is either a *plant* or an *animal*. In Unit 1.4, the students will learn that non-living things can be sorted into those that *once lived* and those that *have never lived*. For this lesson, they do not need to know any of these distinctions, but should be able to identify whether something is living or non-living.

Introduction

- Use the topic opener photograph on Student's Book page 1 as a talking point. Ask the students to describe what they can see. Let them briefly discuss in groups what they know about plants and flowers. Tell them that they are going to learn all about plants in this topic.

- Ask the class to look at the picture on Student's Book page 2. Ask: *What can you see in the picture? Can you suggest some groups you could sort the things in the picture into?* Take feedback but guide the students to select *living* and *non-living* as the criteria.

- Introduce the terms *living* and *non-living* as key words. Ask the students to repeat the words after you. Invite them to give examples of living and non-living things. This will help you assess their prior knowledge and ability to differentiate between living and non-living. Finally, repeat the key words again.

Teaching and learning activities

- Make sure the students understand the questions on Student's Book pages 2–3. Remind them of the two groups: *living* and *non-living*. Ask them to identify all the living and non-living things in the pictures. Then let them discuss their answers in groups. Some students may begin to talk about the similarities and differences they notice between living and non-living things. You can encourage this to develop their interest in the topic but do not correct any misconceptions at this stage. Check the answers as a class.

- Ask the students to cut out pictures of living and non-living things from magazines. Allow them time to freely discuss the pictures with a partner, saying which pictures they chose and why. The pictures can be kept for using on the posters the students will make in the first graded activity.

Graded activities

1 Give each pair of students a large sheet of paper, scissors, glue, coloured pens or pencils and a copy PCM B1, which shows a variety of living and non-living things. Ask the students to sort the pictures into two groups: *living* and *non-living*. Once the sorting is done, ask them to make a poster by sticking the pictures onto the large sheet of paper. Encourage the students to colour in the pictures as this develops fine motor skills and gives practice at holding a pencil. They should write *living* or *non-living* next to each picture. Ask: *Which things are living and which are non-living?* Stick the finished posters on the wall and discuss them with the students.

2 If possible, take the students on a walk around the school grounds. Say: *Count how many living things you can see. Count how many non-living things you can see.* Encourage them to make lists and to classify the objects as being either living or non-living. Ask: *What made you decide if a thing was living or non-living?* (Before the lesson you could 'hide' some living and non-living objects around the school grounds for the students to find.)

3 Show the class Slideshow B1 of living and non-living things and ask: *Which are the living things? Which are the non-living things?* Let them discuss their answers in pairs. Take feedback and invite the class to name each thing in the slideshow, either in English or in their own language. Then ask the students to choose one living thing that they know the name of and to describe it to a partner. Some students may prefer to make their choice from those shown on the slideshow. More able students can choose any appropriate living thing.

Consolidate and review

● Use Workbook page 1 to consolidate the teaching and to check that the students can distinguish between living and non-living things.

● Show the students a doll and ask them to suggest, to a partner, the ways in which they are similar to the doll and the ways in which they are different. Encourage them to conclude that they are living and the doll is non-living. Some students may begin to discuss the characteristics of living things. They will learn more about these in Stage 3 of this course.

Differentiation

■ All of the students should be able to sort the pictures into living and non-living things. Some will be able to do this more quickly than others, but they can move onto the colouring and sticking. More able students may like to add the pictures that they cut from magazines to their poster and should be able to label these correctly. If some students need support with the labelling, write *living* and *non-living* for them to copy.

● Most of the students should be able to identify a selection of living and non-living things during the walk with a little help. If not, demonstrate by showing them a few examples. Most students should be able to record what they see and to organise the things into two lists: one for living and one for non-living. This is useful practice in a method for recording data.

▲ Some of the students should be able to identify the specific examples of living and non-living things and give a detailed description of a living thing of their choice to a partner. Encourage them to describe as many features as possible, for example size, colour and shape. You could turn this into a guessing game by asking students to hide the identity of the living thing they have chosen. Partners should try and guess what it is, based on the description.

Big Cat 🐾

Students who have read *Big Cat The oak tree* may relate the learning in this lesson to the many different types of organism, including plants and animals, described in this book. It provides a lively introduction to the topic of living things.

1.2 Plants and animals are living things

Student's Book pages 4–5

Biology learning objectives

- Know that plants are living things.
- Know that there are living things and things that have never been alive.

Resources

- Workbook page 2
- Video B1: Living and non-living
- PCM B2: Plants or animals? (1 and 2)

Classroom equipment

- large sheets of paper
- coloured pens or pencils
- scissors
- pictures or specimens of plants and animals
- large cards

Scientific enquiry skills

- *Ideas and evidence:* Try to answer questions by collecting evidence through observation.
- *Consider evidence and approach:* Make comparisons.

Key words

- **plant**
- **animal**
- **alive**

 Supervise the students when they use scissors.

Scientific background

Plants and *animals* are *living things*. If something is *alive* it can be seen at this stage as either a plant or an animal. All living things can be sorted into groups according to their features. The two main groups are plants and animals. The sorting of living things into either plant or animal is a very simplistic form of grouping. Students will learn in later stages that these two groups can be divided into smaller groups. For example, animals can be divided into vertebrates and invertebrates, and then further divided into groups such as mammals, birds and fish. Students will also learn in later stages about living things that are neither plant nor animal such as fungi, unicellular organisms and viruses. They do not need to know these detailed classifications yet, but should be able to classify living things into the two basic groups: plants and animals.

Introduction

- Write the key words on the board: *plant*, *animal* and *alive*. Explain that we say a living thing is *alive*. Ask the students to repeat each key word after you. The students should be familiar with the concept of plants and animals in a general sense and be able to name examples of each. Invite individual students to name a plant or animal, in their own language or in English, and write their responses

on the board in two separate lists. Introduce new words as necessary.

- Remind the students that we can classify everything around us into *living* and *non-living*. Show the students Video B1 about living and non-living things. Say: *Can you suggest how you would sort the living things into groups?* Take feedback but guide the students to select *plants* and *animals* as the criteria. Explain that plants and animals are living things: they are alive. Ask the students to say whether each living thing on the video is a plant or an animal. Once they have identified the living things, ask if they know the names of any of the plants and animals, and add these names to your class lists on the board.

- Ask the class to look at the picture on Student's Book pages 4–5. Ask: *Which things in the picture are living? Which are non-living?* Let them discuss this in their groups. Ask: *What made you decide if a thing was living or non-living?* Take feedback and write their responses on the board. Say: *Count how many spiders you can see in the picture. Count how many birds you can see.* Counting the animals out loud will help to reinforce numeracy skills.

Teaching and learning activities

- Have available lots of pictures of animals and plants, or, even better, specimens of the real things. In groups of three, the students should sort them according to their own criteria. As they do so, circulate and check that they are sorting correctly. Ask: *Can you explain how you sorted the plants and animals into groups?* Different groups of students should be challenged to explain why they have grouped things in a particular way.

- Make sure students understand the questions on Student's Book pages 4–5. Discuss the answers as a class. Ask the students how many different types of plants are in the picture and to compare their similarities and differences. Circulate, asking questions to draw out some simple similarities and differences. Ask: *What colour are the plants? Where do the plants live? Are the plants all the same size?*

- Ask: *Can you explain how we know if something is a plant or an animal?* In pairs, ask the students to draw an imaginary animal and to list all the things that it can do. Do not correct any misconceptions at this stage.

- Repeat the exercise with an imaginary plant. The students should be encouraged to think about what colour, shape and size the plant should be. They can also think about where the plant is growing. At this stage, any reasonable suggestions are fine.

Graded activities

1 Give each pair of students a copy of PCM B2. Ask them to cut out the pictures and to sort them into plants and animals. As they do so, circulate and check that they are sorting the pictures correctly. If the pictures are photocopied onto card, they can be used repeatedly. This activity will give you a clear idea of the students' understanding of the grouping of living things.

2 Remind the students about the walk around the school grounds which they did in the previous lesson. Tell them to look back at their list of living things. Ask: *How many living things did you find?* Ask them to write *plant* or *animal* next to each living thing on their list. Some students may be able to name specific plants and animals.

3 Give the students a piece of paper and ask them to draw a line down the middle and label one side 'plants' and the other 'animals'. Then ask them

to draw or write about a plant and an animal that they know. They should describe the features and compare them. The drawings can be fictitious, but the descriptions of the features should be accurate. Ask the students: *Has the plant got legs? Does the animal have more than two eyes?* Discuss with the class why they chose certain features. Explain that when we *compare* things, we look for things that are the same and things that are different. Ask: *In what ways are they the same? In what ways are they different?*

Consolidate and review

- Use Workbook page 2 to consolidate the teaching and to check that the students understand that everything is either living or non-living, and that living things can be grouped into plants or animals.

- Play the 'What am I?' game: you say one clue at a time, with the clues leading to the identity of a familiar plant or animal. The students have to guess what it is. Once the rules are established, the students can play this on their own.

Differentiation

■ All of the students should be able to sort the familiar living things into plants and animals based on obvious criteria.

● Most of the students should be able to identify and correctly label each of the living things on their list as either a plant or an animal, with little prompting. Some may also know the names of the plants and animals that they found.

▲ Some of the students should be able to start comparing similarities and differences between plants and animals by considering their different features. More able students should be able to explain their reasoning in simple terms.

1.3 Plants can grow and move

Student's Book pages 6–7

Biology learning objectives

- Know that plants are living things.
- Know that plants need light and water to grow.

Resources

- Workbook page 3
- Video B2: Plants growing and moving
- PCM B3: Elham and the beans (1 and 2)
- PCM B4: Will it grow?
- DVD Activity B1: Living things

Classroom equipment

- two pots, some stones, cress seeds
- some real plants, some artificial plants, some pictures of plants, two hoops

Note: A few days before this lesson, plant some of the seeds in one of the pots and water regularly, to allow time for the seedlings to appear. Immediately before the lesson, plant some stones in the second pot.

Scientific enquiry skills

- *Plan investigative work*: Make predictions.
- *Obtain and present evidence*: Explore and observe in order to collect evidence (measurements and observations) to answer questions.
- *Consider evidence and approach*: Compare what happened with predictions.

Key words
- **grow**
- **move**

Scientific background

Plants and animals have both similarities and differences. All living things carry out the seven life processes, though they do so in very different ways: they *move*, *respire*, *grow*, *reproduce* (have young), *feed*, *excrete* waste and are *sensitive* to changes in their environment (via their senses). Non-living things do not do these things (for themselves).

At Stage 1, students' main focus will be on characteristics which are familiar to them, such as movement and growth, and learning how plants can do these things. Other characteristics of living things will be taught in more detail in Stage 3 of this course.

Introduction

- Reinforce the students' learning of *living* and *non-living* by asking: *What is the same about a chair and a person?* (They both have legs.) Ask: *Does that mean the chair is a living thing? Why?* Let the students discuss their ideas in groups. Take feedback as a class.

- Next, ask the class: *Can you tell me the differences between living and non-living things?* Take feedback, eliciting ideas such as the table does not *move* or *grow*. Write the responses on the board and ask students to explain their ideas. Ask the others: *Do you agree with these differences?* Encourage them to ask questions.

- Ask the class to look at the picture on Student's Book page 6. Ask them to discuss the different plants they can see. Ask: *Where are the plants? Where else do plants grow? Are the plants living? Explain how you know they are living.* Take feedback from the whole class and establish that the plants are growing.

Teaching and learning activities

- Place two hoops on the floor. Position a variety of real plants, artificial (plastic) plants and pictures of plants outside the hoops. Pick up a real plant, study it carefully for about 5 seconds, and then place it inside one of the hoops. Pick up an artificial plant, study it for about 5 seconds, and then place it in the other hoop. Ask for a volunteer student to put the next plant in the correct hoop. Guide and scaffold the students to continue the activity. Ask them to discuss and explain why they have placed the plants in the different hoops. Then ask them to describe the differences between plants in the different hoops in their groups.

- Ask: *Can you describe to me how we can tell if a plant is living?* Explore the idea that a living plant will grow and need water but non-living things do not. Ask questions to elicit that plants *grow*. More able students may suggest that living things also breathe, have senses and have young. Acknowledge these responses but do not dwell on these characteristics at this stage as they will taught in more detail in Stage 3 of this course. All students should be familiar with some characteristics such as growth. Other concepts will be new to them.

● Display the key words on the board and explain as necessary. Point out how each word is spelled and how it is pronounced. Ask the students to repeat the words after you. Invite individual students to name a living thing (plant or animal) and write their responses on the board. Introduce new words as necessary.

● Make sure students understand the questions on Student's Book pages 6–7. Work through the questions as a class. Their answers should show you how well they have understood the concepts of the lesson.

Graded activities

1 Show the class Video B2 of a plant growing and moving towards the light. Ask: *What is the plant doing?* Take feedback and discuss the students' ideas by encouraging them to ask questions, share ideas from their group and to challenge the ideas of other groups. Establish that the plant is growing and moving, and stress that all plants grow and move. Ask: *What does this tell us about plants?* (They are living things.) More able students may say that plants move to face the Sun.

2 Read the story from PCM B3. Let the students discuss it. Ask: *Has anyone done what Elham did? What happened?* Let the students recount their own experiences. Return to the story and ask: *What happened to the bean seed?* (It grew into a plant.) *What direction did it grow?* (up) *If the plant can grow and move, what does this tell us about it?* (It is living.) At this stage, do not focus on the detail of the plant parts or how the plant grew from a seed. The purpose of the activity is to reinforce that plants are alive and how we know this.

3 Give each student a copy of PCM B4. Say that you planted some seeds in one pot and some stones in another. Ask: *What do you think has happened?* Say that you have been watering both pots. Ask: *Will this have changed what happened? Why do you think this?* Allow the students to discuss this in groups. Ask them to draw each pot on PCM B4. They should try to explain why the

seeds have grown but the stones did not. (The seeds are living and the stones are non-living.) Tell the students: *Saying what you think has happened is called making a prediction.*

Consolidate and review

● Use Workbook page 3 to consolidate the teaching so far. Check that the students understand some simple characteristics of living things, and that they know that both plants and animals have these characteristics but that non-living things do not.

● Let the students complete DVD Activity B1 to consolidate their learning.

Differentiation

■ All of the students should be able to describe that the plant is growing and moving. More able students may talk about the plant growing towards and moving towards the light. Students should be able to understand that this therefore means that the plant is alive.

● Most of the students should be able to understand that the bean seeds grew into a plant and that the plant is a living thing, with just a little help. If not, ask questions to guide them to the correct conclusion. Some will be able to explain their reasoning more accurately and in more detail.

▲ Some of the students should be able to correctly predict the outcome of the investigation – that the seeds will have grown but the stones will not – but they may need help to explain their reasoning. With some support, the students should be able to draw a representation of their prediction.

1.4 Things that have never been alive

Student's Book pages 8–9

Biology learning objective
- Know that there are living things and things that have never been alive.

Resources
- Workbook pages 4 and 5

Classroom equipment
- scissors
- glue
- selection of old magazines

Scientific enquiry skills
- *Ideas and evidence:* Try to answer questions by collecting evidence through observation.
- *Consider evidence and approach*: Make comparisons.

Key words
- **non-living**   • **alive**   • **living**

⚠ Supervise the students when they use scissors. If the students explore things around the classroom, make sure they do so safely.

Scientific background

Everything in the world can be sorted into *living* or *non-living*. All living things carry out the *seven life processes*: they move, respire, grow, reproduce (have young), feed, excrete waste and are sensitive to changes in their environment (via their senses). Non-living things do not do these things (for themselves). As with living things, non-living things can be divided into groups. They can be grouped into those which *once lived* and therefore carried out the seven life processes, such as wood used for furniture, and those which *have never lived*, such as stone. Non-living things that once lived come from *natural* sources, such as cotton and fruit from plants, and wool and leather from animals. Things that have never lived can also be found in nature, but many are *manufactured*, such as metal, glass and plastic. Students do not need to differentiate between natural and manufactured materials at this stage, but they should be able to classify non-living things into those that *once lived* and those that *have never lived*.

Introduction

- Review the previous lesson by asking questions relating to the differences between living and non-living things. Ask the class: *In what ways are all living things the same?* Take feedback and make a class list of all their ideas on the board. Choose an object that is definitely living, such as a horse, and check each of the ideas on the board. If one of the criteria is true for the horse, put a tick. If it is not true, cross it out. Choose another living thing but, this time, choose something that you know will clear a few more misconceptions, such as a butterfly, then a sunflower. Continue until all the misconceptions have been crossed off.

- Ask the students to look at the scene in the picture on Student's Book pages 8–9. Ask the class questions and guide them to the correct answers: *Where was the wood in the logs before they were used to build the hut?* (on a tree) *What was the tree doing?* (growing) *Was the wood alive?* (Yes) *Are the logs growing now?* (No) *What does this tell us?* (They are non-living but were once alive.).

Teaching and learning activities

- Explain that some things have never been alive and illustrate this point with plenty of examples. Tell students that they can work out whether something has been alive or not by checking it against their list of criteria for living things. If the object has never done any of the things on the list, then it has never been alive.

- Make sure the students understand the questions on Student's Book page 9. Then let them discuss their answers in groups. They should identify the non-living things in the picture and then classify these into *once lived* and *has never lived*. Circulate, offering support and guidance as necessary. Check the answers as a class. Ask the students to explain their reasoning as fully as possible.

- Identify any misconceptions that the students may have; for example, some students may think that wood is living. Explain: *Wood was once living, but when it is cut from a tree it is no longer growing, so is no longer living.*

Graded activities

1 Let the students complete the activity on Workbook page 4. They should circle all the non-living things that have never been alive. Some students may need help distinguishing between non-living things that were once alive, such as wood, and things that have never been alive, such as the television. Circulate, asking questions to guide them as necessary, e.g. ask: *Where did the vegetable come from? Was it alive when it was part of the plant? Is it alive now?* When the students have completed the task, ask them to name the non-living things, either in English or in their own language.

2 Ask the students to walk around the classroom. Tell them: *Look for some things that were once living. Look for some things that have never been alive.* Ask them to make a list of as many things as they can. (Before the lesson you could 'hide' some once living and never lived objects around classroom for the students to find.) This activity should show how well the students have understood the difference between the two categories of non-living things.

3 Put students in pairs or small groups and give them some old magazines, scissors and glue. Ask them to make an odd-one-out poster by cutting and sticking pictures of things that were once alive and things that have never been alive. Explain that they should choose several objects from one group and only one from the other group. The students should also suggest why the object is the odd one out, and write this on the back of their poster. Use this activity to assess their reasoning. When they have completed their posters, let other groups try to identify the odd one out.

Consolidate and review

- Use Workbook page 5 to consolidate the teaching and to check that the students understand the difference between living things and non-living things which have never been alive.

- Ask the students: *Can you explain how we know that we are living? What do we do that a doll does not do? What does a flower do that we do?* Allow them time to discuss their ideas in groups. Take feedback and accept any suitable answers.

Differentiation

■ All of the students should be able to identify the non-living things that have never been alive with little prompting. If not, help the students by reminding them of some of the criteria of living things and asking whether each object ever did those things.

● Most of the students should be able to identify a selection of once alive and never been alive things. Most students should be able to record what they see and organise the data in two lists: one for once alive and one for never been alive. This is useful practice in a method for recording data.

▲ Some of the students should be able to independently choose a selection of once alive pictures and one never been alive picture, or vice versa. They should be able to work collaboratively, to think creatively and correctly sort objects into groups, and then explain their reasoning.

1.5 Plant and animal homes

Student's Book pages 10–11

Biology learning objective

- Explore ways that different animals and plants inhabit local environments.

Resources

- Workbook pages 6 and 7
- Slideshow B2: Leaves
- Video B3: Penguins huddling together
- Video B4: Polar bears
- PCM B5: Five little leaves

Classroom equipment

- coloured pens or pencils
- large sheets of paper
- different types of leaves
- reference materials on polar bears
- world map or globe

Note: Before the lesson, research some information about polar bears and their environment.

Scientific enquiry skills

- *Ideas and evidence:* Try to answer questions by collecting evidence through observation.
- *Plan investigative work:* Ask questions and contribute to discussions about how to seek answers.
- *Consider evidence and approach:* Make comparisons.

Key words

- **environment**

 If the students use the internet, ensure they do so safely and under adult supervision.

Scientific background

We use the term *environment* to talk about our surroundings. There are many different types of environments around the world, and different plants and animals inhabit them. A suitable environment is essential for the survival of any plant or animal. Ideally, the environment will supply the animals that live there with food, clean water, air, and shelter from the weather and predators. Plants need to have access to light and water.

Plants come in different shapes, sizes and colours, and each type of plant is suited to its environment. Animals are also suited to the conditions of the environment that they live in. For example, animals that live in hot climates have specific behaviour patterns to enable them to cool down, such as burrowing underground or being nocturnal. Animals that live in cold climates can migrate or hibernate. Some grow thick coats of fur to keep warm through the winter and then shed this coat when the weather warms up again.

The students will learn more about the adaptation of plants and animals to their environment in Stage 2. At this stage, they need to understand that there is a wide range of different environments, and that different plants and animals inhabit them.

Introduction

- Talk briefly to the class about their homes. Ask: *What is a home? Why do we need homes?* Establish that a home is a place where we can eat and sleep, where we are protected from the weather and from being harmed. Tell the students that plants and animals also need homes.

- Introduce *environment* as a key word. Explain that we use the word *environment* to describe our surroundings. Introduce some more key words: *hot, cold, wet, dry, land, water,* and say that we can use these words to describe different environments. Make sure the students understand what these words mean.

- Ask the class to look at the pictures on Student's Book page 10. Ask: *What do you think it is like in these environments? Do you think the same plants and animals live in these environments?* Take feedback and guide the students to establish that different plants and animals live in different types of environments. At this stage, the students do not need to be any more specific than this.

Teaching and learning activities

- Show the class two very different shaped leaves and ask the students to draw them. Ask: *What differences can you see between the two leaves?* Ask the students to think of a sentence about each leaf. It can be about anything relevant: shape, colour, size, appearance, texture. Help them to write their sentences, supplying suitable adjectives if necessary.

- Show the class Slideshow B2, of trees and leaves with different shapes and colours. Discuss that there is a huge variety of plants which live in all types of environments. Explain in very simple terms that each plant must be suited to live in its environment, otherwise it would not survive.

- Ask the students: *What do animals need to live?* Write the students' suggestions on the board. Ensure that their suggestions include: food, water, warmth and safety. Ask: *What do you do if you feel very cold? What can animals do if they get cold? They do not have clothes and blankets.* Explain that some animals curl into balls or huddle together to keep warm. Show Video B3 of penguins huddling together. Ask: *Why do you think they do this? What do the penguins do to keep warm?* Explain that this is an example of animals huddling together to share body warmth in a cold environment.

- Make sure the students understand the questions on Student's Book page 11. Take feedback and discuss the answers as a class.

Graded activities

1 Let the students complete the activity on Workbook page 6. They should match each plant to the environment that it lives in. As they do this, you can ask them to describe the different environments: *snowy*, *underwater*, *temperate*, *hot desert*. Circulate, asking questions to guide their thinking.

2 Give each student a large sheet of paper and some coloured pens or pencils. Ask the students to draw their favourite animal. It can be from anywhere in the world, but the students should be familiar with it. Once their drawing is complete, the students should describe the animal and say where it lives. Students can then work in pairs to compare the animals they have chosen.

3 Show the class Video B4 of a polar bear. Explain that the polar bear is an endangered animal.

Ask the students to describe where a polar bear lives. (Arctic regions, where it is very cold with lots of snow and ice) Explain that polar bears need the sea ice to survive because this is where they hunt for their food (seals). Next, ask the students for ideas about what might cause a threat to the polar bear. Ask: *What would happen if the polar bears did not have any food?* Explain that polar bears are under threat due to destruction of their environment: a reduction in sea ice due to global warming. Although the science behind this is too advanced for students at this stage, they should be able to understand that less sea ice means less food and fewer polar bears. If appropriate, help the students to do some further research using reference books or the internet. Students should work in groups to make a fact sheet to illustrate their findings. Display these on the wall in the classroom and discuss. Ask: *What could we do to try to help the polar bears?* Accept all suitable answers.

Consolidate and review

- Use Workbook page 7 to consolidate the teaching and to check that the students understand that different plants and animals live in different types of environments.

- Teach the students the *Five little leaves* action rhyme, from PCM B5, and help them to recognise the rhythm and repeating action.

Differentiation

■ All of the students should be able to correctly match each plant to the environment that it lives in.

● Most of the students should be able to draw a reasonable representation of their chosen animal and then give an accurate description. Some will be able to give more detailed descriptions than others. You may need to offer prompts if any students struggle to explain what the animal looks like and where it lives.

▲ Some of the students should be able to understand the threats to the polar bear's environment. Some will work collaboratively, thinking critically and asking sensible questions to extend their knowledge. More able students will be able to recognise the implications and potential outcome if nothing is done to help protect the bears.

1.6 Different environments

Student's Book pages 12–13

Biology learning objective
- Explore ways that different animals and plants inhabit local environments.

Resources
- Workbook page 8
- Slideshow B3: Jungle environments
- Slideshow B4: Plants in different places
- PCM B6: Plants I can see

Classroom equipment
- large sheets of paper, coloured pens or pencils
- world map or globe
- hand lenses
- cacti and desert plants
- map of the school grounds

Scientific enquiry skills
- *Ideas and evidence:* Try to answer questions by collecting evidence through observation.

Key words
- **desert**
- **rainforest**
- **mountains**
- **underwater**

⚠ If you take the students on an investigative walk, ensure they are safe when they are in the school grounds. Take care if handling cacti.

Scientific background

Plants can be found in almost every type of environment. Deserts are the driest of all environments and make up approximately 20% of the Earth's land surface. They have few plants and very little rain. There are hot deserts and cold deserts. Hot deserts are very hot during the day but can be extremely cold at night. Approximately 70% of the Earth's surface is covered by water and more than 97% of this water is salt water. The ocean environment is divided into different zones, according to how much sunlight reaches the zone. There are many different kinds of forest around the world, for example tropical rainforests, temperate rainforests, boreal forests and mangrove forests.

Wherever they live, plants need water, air and light. The features of a plant make it suited to the environment that it lives in. Plants such as cacti can store water in their thick and fleshy leaves and stems, so are suited to environments such as deserts where there is little water available. Tropical rainforests have dense vegetation so very little sunlight penetrates to the forest floor. Plants are adapted to this by growing on other plants or by climbing round other plants so they can reach sunlight. Plants that grow in tundra or arctic places have to cope with fierce winds or year-round snowstorms. They have hairs and are clumped together to keep warm, and are small and low-growing.

At this stage, the students only need to understand that plants can be found in a wide range of environments, and that different plants prefer to live in different environments.

Introduction

- Ask the students: *What types of living things would you find in an underwater environment? Why are some plants and animals able to live in very cold, snowy environments?* Allow them to discuss their ideas in groups. Take feedback and establish that different plants and animals live in different environments, and that most prefer to live in one environment more than another. Tell the students that they are now going to learn more about plants that grow in different environments.

- Show Slideshow B3 of jungle environments and discuss with the students the characteristics of the plants, e.g. lots of tall trees with creepers growing on them, shady. List the students' responses on the board.

- Write the key words on the board. Ask questions to elicit what each type of environment is like. Ask: *What is a desert?* (a dry area with very little rainfall) Point out that cold deserts also exist, in the polar regions.

- Ask the class to look at the pictures on Student's Book pages 12–13. Ask: *What do you think each environment is like?*

Teaching and learning activities

- Let the class watch Slideshow B4, of plants growing in hot deserts and in cold, snowy areas. *Ask: Are all of the plants similar? Do they have similar features?* Let the students discuss their ideas in their groups. Take feedback, one point from each group in turn. Write their ideas on the board. Repeat the exercise, asking: *Are all of the plants different?* Summarise by explaining that plants all have some things in common but they are different because they have features that help them to live in different environments.

- Give the students magnifying lenses and let them look closely at a variety of cacti and other desert plants. Remove a cactus from the pot and show the students the roots. The different parts of a plant and their functions will be introduced later in the topic. At this stage, the students do not need to understand the jobs that roots do, but some more able students may know that they are called 'roots'. Let them discuss what they can see, in small groups, then report back to the whole class.

- Make sure students understand the questions on Student's Book pages 12–13. Work through the answers as a class. Encourage the students to give reasons for their answers.

Graded activities

1 Let the students complete the activity on Workbook page 8. They should tick the names of the plants and animals that live in each environment. As they do this, you can ask them to describe the different environments: *grasslands, alpine (temperate mountains), desert, rainforest.* Circulate, asking questions to guide their thinking: *Is it cold there? Would a polar bear like to live in a hot environment?*

2 Give each student a copy of PCM B6. The students should record the plants by drawing pictures on PCM B6. Support the students in identifying the names of different plants as necessary. Ask about plants that are similar to those they have identified. Then ask about plants that live in similar places, for example ask: *What other plants might live near the school?*

3 Tell the students they are going to make a class display of the plants found in the local environment around your school. Take them on a walk around the school grounds. Ask: *Are all of the*

plants similar? Are they different?* Elicit differences in size, shape and colour. Some students may begin to discuss specific parts of the plants. They will learn more about this later in the topic. Back in the classroom, the students should draw a picture of a plant that they particularly liked and describe where it lives. Have a large prepared map of the school grounds and ask the students to locate their plant on the map.

Consolidate and review

- Ask the students about the types of plants and animals they would find in a particular environment, for example ask: *Can you count how many different types of plants and animals you can name that live in the sea?* Let them discuss this in pairs.

- Ask the students to look around at their classmates. Ask: *Do we all look the same?* Explain that, just as we all look different, plants and animals of the same type also have differences as well. (Students will learn more about similarities and differences between humans in the next topic.)

Differentiation

■ All of the students should be able to identify which plants and animals live in each of the different environments. Some may find this easier than others. Circulate, asking questions if the students need some guidance.

● Most of the students should be able to select a plant from home and a plant which they saw on the way to school. Some may find it difficult to draw accurately from memory. The drawings themselves are not as important as the students being able to give an accurate description of where the plant lives. Write some suitable adjectives on the board to help if necessary.

▲ Some of the students should be able to think critically to name similarities and differences between plants in the local environment and accurately draw a picture of one of them, giving a detailed description of where it lives. More able students may suggest why it lives there.

1.7 Exploring local environments

Student's Book pages 14–15

Biology learning objective

- Explore ways that different animals and plants inhabit local environments.

Resources

- Workbook pages 9 and 10

Classroom equipment

- map of the school grounds
- paper
- video equipment
- various large leaves
- paint

Scientific enquiry skills

- *Plan investigative work:* Ask questions and contribute to discussions about how to seek answers; make predictions; decide what to do to try to answer a science question.
- *Obtain and present evidence:* Explore and observe in order to collect evidence (measurements and observations) to answer questions; record stages in work.
- *Consider evidence and approach:* Compare what happened with predictions; model and communicate ideas in order to share, explain and develop them.

Key words

- **local environment**

⚠ Students should conduct their outdoor investigation under careful supervision. Ensure they are safe when they are in the school grounds. They should not put anything they find into their mouths. Take care not to let students pick up unsavoury items from the ground. Remind students to wash their hands when they have finished exploring the outdoor areas. Supervise the students when they use paint.

Scientific background

Plants can be found in almost every type of environment. Our *local environment* is the area closest to us. There are often smaller localised areas with varied conditions, for example areas of sun, shade, dryness and damp, all within a given local environment. As the features of a plant or animal make it suited to the environment that it lives in, different living things can be found in different local environments. In this lesson, the students will do a detailed investigation into the local environment around your school.

Introduction

- Introduce *local environment* as a key term and ask the students what they think it means. Write the students' suggestions on the board. Guide them to elicit that it refers to the environment close to us. If the students are unfamiliar with the terms, introduce the words *sunny* and *shady* at this point too. Make sure the students understand what these words mean.
- Ask the students to consider the local environment around your school. Ask: *What is the environment like? What plants and animals might you find there?* Do they think they might find a sunflower or a bat? If not, why not? Make sure the students know that some animals will not come out if humans are about.
- Ask the students to describe the plants they saw in the school grounds in the previous lesson. If you do not have school grounds, ask them to talk about a park or wood that they have visited. Make a class list of all the plants and animals that they know live in the area immediately outside the school.

Teaching and learning activities

- Ask the students to look at the pictures on Student's Book page 14. Ask them to look at the pictures and describe the woodland and the examples of local areas that can often be found there. Make sure the students understand the questions and let them discuss their answers in groups. Say: *Count how many different types of plants you can see. Do you think any animals live inside the logs?* Take feedback and then discuss their ideas as a class.

- Show the class the picture on Student's Book page 15. Explain that they are going to do a detailed investigation to find out what plants and animals can be found in the local environment around their school. Because students will be dealing with living things, make a class list for an acceptable code of conduct and discuss why the students must adhere to it. Ask: *What should we do to make sure we keep the plants and animals safe? What should we not do?* Write the ideas on the board and keep them there for referring back to later in the lesson.

- In groups, ask the students to make a list of all the different types of areas they can think of within the school grounds. Encourage students to consider less obvious areas such as under stones, logs, leaves, etc. Take suggestions and make a list on the board. Ensure that it includes as wide a range of different conditions as possible.

Graded activities

1 Tell the students to think of some different areas within the local environment around your school, for example a shady area under some trees, or a sunny area in the middle of a playing field, or a damp area under some rocks. If possible, the students should compile their own list, but if they cannot do this they should be directed by you. Ask: *What plants and animals do you think you will find there? Why?* Ask them to draw and write what they would expect to find on Workbook page 9. Students should try and explain reasons for why they expect to find those things in each area. To help them do this, circulate asking: *Where do flowers like to live? Would a mouse like to live there? Where would a spider like to make its web?*

2 Ask the students to work in groups to plan how they can find out which living things inhabit their local environment. Encourage them to think about what they will do and how they will take care not to damage or disturb the plants and animals. Refer them back to your class code of conduct. Once they have finalised their plans, check that they are suitable and then take the students for a walk around the school grounds. They should make an in-depth survey of their local environment by observing as many areas as possible, turning over leaves, looking under logs and stones, etc. Students should record what they observe and where on Workbook page 10.

3 Back in the classroom, the groups should discuss their findings. Then invite groups to present their findings to the rest of the class. Encourage the students to use as much detail as possible to describe what they found. Put a large prepared map of the grounds on the board. Ask the students to locate their plants and animals on the map. To finish, they should decide whether their findings matched their predictions or not.

Consolidate and review

- Ask the students to produce an information sheet or brochure, describing the exciting things that can be found in the local environment around your school. Their target audience could be another Stage 1 student.

- If appropriate, the students could make a video of their walk. This could be shown in assembly to support environmental work.

- Let the students use large leaves and paint to make leaf prints. Discuss with the students the different shapes of the leaves and their different edge patterns.

Differentiation

■ All of the students should be able to suggest a range of plants and animals they would expect to find in the local environment around your school. Some will be able to name less obvious examples. Most should be able to make predictions and explain their reasoning with a little prompting.

● Most of the students should be able to plan how they can investigate a local environment, working collaboratively, and asking and answering questions to clarify their thinking. Most of the students should be able to draw a reasonably accurate diagram from first-hand observations with some support.

▲ Some of the students should be able to work together, challenging each other by asking questions. Some should be able to construct simple sentences to describe what they observed and then accurately assess whether this matched their predictions or not. Some may not be able to do this yet, in which case you may prefer to offer a more structured framework for the activity.

1.8 **Parts of a plant**

Student's Book pages 16–17

Biology learning objective

- Name the major parts of a plant, looking at real plants and models.

Resources

- Workbook pages 11 and 12
- Slideshow B5: Leaves and flowers
- Slideshow B6: Fruit and vegetables
- DVD Activity B2: Plant parts

Classroom equipment

- variety of leaves
- variety of plants or flowers
- glue, colouring pens or pencils, large sheets of paper
- variety of edible roots
- paper and wax crayons

Scientific enquiry skills

- *Obtain and present evidence:* Explore and observe in order to collect evidence (measurements and observations) to answer questions.
- *Consider evidence and approach:* Model and communicate ideas in order to share, explain and develop them.

Key words

- **root**
- **leaf**
- **fruit**
- **stem**
- **flower**

⚠️ The vegetables must be clean and fresh. The students should not eat any plant parts unless supervised. Some leaves can cause irritation. Some students may have allergies to some types of pollen. Warn students not to rub their eyes or faces and not to put their fingers near their mouths. Make sure they wash their hands after handling the plants.

Scientific background

All flowering plants have the same parts. The *leaves* use energy from the Sun, carbon dioxide and water to make food for the plant (glucose) and oxygen. *Roots* have two functions: they anchor the plant securely in the soil and absorb water and other nutrients. Most roots grow underground. The *stem* transports the water and nutrients around the plant, similar to an animal's circulatory system. The stem also holds the plant upright. *Flowers* form the *fruit* which contain the *seeds* in a plant, though not all plants produce flowers.

Different plants have different kinds of roots. Some plants have *fibrous roots* and other plants have *tap roots*. The tap root may have smaller branches growing off it. Some tap roots, such as carrots, are edible. At this stage, students should know that different plants have different types of roots but they do not need to know their names.

At Stage 1 the students only need to be able to identify and name the major parts of a plant. They do not to need to know about the roles of the different plant plants, they will learn more about these in Stage 3 of this course.

Introduction

- Ask the students: *What do you know about plants?* Encourage them to take turns to share their opinions and listen to the opinions of the others in the group. Write their ideas on the board.

- Show the students a variety of plants or a bunch of assorted flowers, with different colours, sizes, scents, number of leaves. Ask the students to examine the flowers, investigating their colours, scent, feel, number of leaves. As a class, discuss and compare the plants in turn. Ask the students to comment about the colour, texture and leaves, asking questions to guide them: *Are all the plants the same colour? Do the flowers smell the same? Are all the leaves big?* Draw the plants on the board and write the students' comments alongside each drawing.

Teaching and learning activities

- Ask the class to look at the pictures on Student's Book page 16. Introduce the different parts of a plant as key terms: *stem, root, leaf, flower* and *fruit.* Write the words on the board and point out the spelling and pronunciation. Ask students to point to each part. Make the distinction between the name of the whole plant and its parts, e.g. an orchid flower and an orchid plant. Ask the students to make a list of the similarities and differences between the two plants. Remind the students that when we look to see how things are the same and how they are different, we say we are *comparing* them.

● Show the students Slideshow B5 of different leaves and flowers. Pause the slideshow after each image to allow the students time to discuss each question in groups. This activity encourages the students to start thinking about the fact that plants have parts that are the same, but that the parts can look very different from one plant to the next.

● Ask the students to look at the pictures on Student's Book page 17. Discuss the plant roots and answer the questions as a whole class. Ensure that the students understand that the carrot and the radish are roots that have grown large. Have some root vegetables and fibrous roots available for them to handle and look at. Ask the students what root vegetables they know about, e.g. sweet potato. Establish that some plants have roots we can eat.

● Talk about plants that we can eat and ask the students to name some. Move on to discuss the fact that not all plants can be eaten and some are poisonous. Explain that we should never eat a plant unless we know that it is good to eat.

Graded activities

1 Let the students complete the activity on Workbook page 11. Circulate and suggest adjectives if the students need prompting. This activity helps to illustrate that plants have the same parts, but that there are differences between these parts. It also helps the students to practise their observational skills.

2 Let the students complete the activity on Workbook page 12. Circulate, asking questions to guide students, e.g. *What is this plant part called?* This activity reinforces the names of the different parts of a plant.

3 Take the students outside to look at a tree, (or have pictures of trees available if this is not possible). Ask: *Can you show me the stem of the tree?* This question will stretch some students and they may identify the branches or leaf stems instead of the trunk. Explain that the 'trunk' of a

tree is its stem. It is just a lot bigger than most plant stems. Let the students sketch a tree of their choice and label the parts. They can also make rubbings of the leaves and bark using paper and wax crayons. If the students make a variety of different rubbings, they can use these to quiz each other to see if they can identify which tree it comes from. Talk about the many different types of trees, but make sure that the students understand they are all plants despite the differences in their size and shape.

Consolidate and review

● Make a poster of an imaginary tree using real leaves. Provide the students with a trunk and branches made from paper. Ask the students to collect leaves from the school grounds or home. The leaves can be stuck to the branches to produce the 'class tree'.

● Show the students Slideshow B6, of various named fruits and vegetables. Say the name of each fruit or vegetable, as it is displayed. Ask: *Who can make a sentence describing the fruit/vegetable?*

● Let the students complete DVD Activity B2 to consolidate their learning.

Differentiation

■ All of the students should be able to suggest a range of differences between two plants of their choice, such as colour and shape. More able students should be able to name less obvious differences, such as smell and texture.

● Most of the students should be able to draw a flowering plant and correctly label the key features: stem, roots, leaves, flower.

▲ Some of the students should be able to say that the trunk of a tree is a stem. They will be able to make an accurate drawing of their tree and label the parts correctly without any help.

Big Cat 🐾

Students who read *Big Cat What's inside?* will have an overview of what is inside living things, including plant parts, animals and humans.

1.9 **What do plants need to grow?**

Student's Book pages 18–19

Biology learning objective

• Know that plants need light and water to grow.

Resources

• Workbook pages 13, 14 and 15
• Video B5: Roots growing

Classroom equipment

• large sheets of paper, coloured pens or pencils
• potted plant
• two bean plants

Note: A few days before the lesson, set up two identical bean plants for the investigation. Give both plants the same amount of water but keep one in the light and one in the dark. Label them 'Light investigation'.

Scientific enquiry skills

• *Plan investigative work:* Ask questions and contribute to discussions about how to seek answers; make predictions; decide what to do to try to answer a science question.
• *Obtain and present evidence:* Explore and observe in order to collect evidence (measurements and observations) to answer questions; suggest ideas and follow instructions; record stages in work.
• *Consider evidence and approach:* Compare what happened with predictions.

Key words

• **water**
• **light**
• **air**
• **soil**

Scientific background

The great majority of plants can make their own food, which they need in order to live and grow well. The green parts of a plant make the food by the process of *photosynthesis*. Water and light are essential for photosynthesis and therefore essential for a plant to live and grow. Plants' leaves turn naturally towards the light. As plants grow, they get bigger and develop more leaves. Plants grown without light are often tall, thin and pale. They are not strong plants. Without water, plants droop or wilt. If they go without water for too long, they will die. At Stage 1 the students do not need to know the details of photosynthesis, but they do need to understand that all plants need water and light to live and grow. The students will learn about photosynthesis in Stages 5 and 6 of this course.

In this lesson, the students will do a class investigation to observe how light affects the growth of plants.

Introduction

● Ask the students: *What do you remember about plants?* Give them a few minutes to discuss this in their groups. Encourage them to take turns to share their opinions and listen to the opinions of the others in the group. Take feedback. Encourage the students to discuss their ideas with the class.

● Review the previous lesson by drawing a picture of a plant on the board. Add labels by eliciting the names of the different parts from the class.

● Tell the class that they are now going to learn more about the things which plants need to live and grow well. Introduce the key terms: *water*, *light*, *air* and *soil*. Write the words on the board and point out the spelling and pronunciation.

Teaching and learning activities

● Ask the class to look at the pictures on Student's Book page 18. Ask the students about the differences between the plants, and why they think the plants are different. Allow them to discuss their ideas in groups and then take feedback. Establish that one tomato plant is healthy and the other two are unhealthy.

● Show the class Video B5 of roots growing. Ask: *What happens to the roots as the plants grow?* Most students will realise that the roots also grow. Some may comment that the roots grow and move downwards.

● Show the students a potted plant. Take it out of the pot to show its roots. Ask the class to observe the colour of the roots and how the roots have grown. Ask: *What do you think plants need in order to grow?* Allow the students to discuss this in groups. Take feedback and write their ideas on the board.

● Explain that plants need water to survive, just like we do. Ask: *What does your mouth and body feel like when you need water? What happens if you cannot find water?* Say that plants also need light to live and grow. Explain, in very simple terms, that plants make their own food. Stress the importance of light (usually from the Sun) and water so they can do this. Without water and light, plants will die. Encourage the students to give their opinions, and to ask and answer questions. Address any misconceptions the students may have about plant food coming from the soil.

Graded activities

1 Explain to the students that they are going to make a poster called 'What plants need to grow'. Ask the students, in their groups, to make posters showing everything they know about plants and what plants need in order to live and grow well. Circulate, asking questions to ensure that the students include all the key features. Display the posters on the wall. Let the students take turns to look at the posters. Ask the students to say what is good about each poster. If appropriate, they can also point out any mistakes and say how the posters could have been even better. This activity should show how well the students have understood the unit.

2 Tell students they are going to explore how light affects the growth of a plant. Show them a healthy bean plant (the one you have been keeping in the light). Ask: *Can you describe how light affects the growth of plants?* Explain that you have been giving two identical plants the same amount of water but keeping one in the light and one in the dark. Ask: *What do you think has happened?* Students should draw the plant you showed them, on Workbook page 13, and work in pairs to predict what has happened to the plant that did not get any light.

3 Show the students the two bean plants. Remind them that you gave both plants the same amount of water but kept one in the light and one in the dark. Ask: *Can you describe how the plants are different? What has changed? Why has this happened?* Ask the students to observe the effects of lack of light and to record their observations on Workbook page 14. Discuss the students' ideas and establish that plants need light to make food and therefore to grow well and be

healthy. Ask: *Which is the healthiest plant? Why?* Encourage the students to explain their reasoning as fully as possible.

Consolidate and review

● Use Workbook page 15 to consolidate the teaching and to check that the students understand the things which plants need in order to live and grow well, in particular the importance of water and light.

● Ask the students to work in pairs to tell each other what plants need to live and grow well.

Differentiation

■ All of the students should be able to work together to share ideas in their groups, asking and answering simple questions and supporting each other, to produce a poster about the needs of a plant.

● Most of the students should be able to make and draw their predictions with a little support. Most should be able to work collaboratively with a partner to help clarify their thinking. Some may find making predictions easier than others, so circulate to offer support as necessary.

▲ Some of the students should be able to compare the two plants and think critically to name the differences. Some should be able to accurately describe the results and explain the outcome in simple terms. Some may struggle to link the lack of light with poor growth. If so, help by reminding the class about what plants need to live and grow well.

1.10 Seeds grow into plants

Student's Book pages 20–21

Biology learning objective
• Explore how seeds grow into flowering plants.

Resources
• Workbook page 16
• Video B6: Plants growing
• Slideshow B7: Bean seedlings
• PCM B7: Comparing seeds
• PCM B8: Plant heads

Classroom equipment
• collection of different fruits, knife, plates
• variety of seeds, e.g. coconut, sunflower, pumpkin, squash, linseed, mango, coriander, mustard, sesame, dandelion
• sticky tape
• bean seedlings in pots, hand lenses, paper towels, string, scissors
• clean, small yogurt pots (one for each student plus four for the teacher), cotton wool, mustard or garden cress seeds, kitchen towel, paint and brushes

Note: In advance of this lesson, prepare some seedlings, staggering the planting so that various stages of germination and growth are available. When the students make their 'plant heads', make four yourself and keep these in varying conditions (watered and light, watered and dark, not watered and light, not watered and dark) for students to examine in the next lesson.

Scientific enquiry skills
• *Ideas and evidence:* Try to answer questions by collecting evidence through observation.
• *Plan investigative work:* Make predictions.
• *Obtain and present evidence:* Explore and observe in order to collect evidence (measurements and observations) to answer questions; record stages in work.
• *Consider evidence and approach:* Compare what happened with predictions.

Key words
• **seed**   • **fruit**   • **seedling**
• **water**   • **warmth**

⚠️ Ensure that students do not eat any of the fruit or seeds. Remind the students to wash their hands after handling them. Do not use examples which are poisonous. Some children may have allergies to nuts. Ensure that students use the hand lenses out of direct sunlight to avoid magnifying bright light that could damage their eyes.

Scientific background

Plants grow from *seeds*. Most seeds will germinate (grow) without *light*, but will not germinate without *water*. Seeds are surrounded by a protective covering, the seed coat. The seed absorbs water, and eventually the seed coat bursts and the tip of the *root* of the new plant emerges. Once a seed begins to sprout, the roots search for water; a *seedling* deprived of water will quickly die. The roots grow downwards and the shoots move upwards. The roots anchor the seed in place, and enable nutrients and water to be absorbed from the soil. The shoot needs light to turn green and grow into a healthy plant. Plants need light to make their food by a process called *photosynthesis,* and they naturally position their leaves so that they can absorb the maximum amount of light. Three factors are required for successful germination: *water, oxygen* and *warmth*, though at this stage the students need to understand the importance of water only.

Introduction

● Ask: *What do you think plants can do?* Take feedback. Write any key words, such as *grow, make seeds*, etc. on the board. Show the students Video B6, a time-lapse recording of seeds growing. Ask them to describe what is happening. Encourage them to ask and answer questions to clarify their thinking.

● Broaden the discussion to lead the class to the idea that all plants grow and change as they get older. Ask: *Can you describe how a plant changes as it grows? Do we change as we grow?* Bring out the similarities and the differences in how all living things grow.

Teaching and learning activities

- Ask the students to look at the pictures on Student's Book page 20 and talk about the different types of seeds they can see. Tell them that some fruits have a small seed and some have a large stone-like seed, and that nuts are seeds. Explain that plants produce seeds and these grow into new plants.

- Show the students a seed from a local plant or tree, both in and out of its coating. Ask: *Do you know what it is?* Have a variety of seeds (including a coconut) available, to show to the class, but do not let the students touch them unless they are wearing plastic gloves. Explain that these are all seeds. Ask: *Why do plants need seeds?* Then ask the students to select some criteria and sort the seeds according to their criteria. Ask them to discuss what they know about seeds.

- Show the students Slideshow B7 of seedlings at different stages of development. Ask: *What does the seed need to grow? Why do the roots grow first? Describe how it changes as it grows.* Pause the slideshow when parts of the plant are shown, and ask the students to name them.

- Ask the students to look at the picture on Student's Book page 21. Ask: *What are the children doing?* Establish that they are planting seeds. Ask: *Have you ever planted some seeds at home? What do you have to do to look after your plants? What do you do to keep the plants healthy?* Encourage the students to share their experiences.

Graded activities

1 Give each student a copy of PCM B7. Provide a wide variety of fruits for them to investigate. Show each whole fruit in turn and ask the students to say where the seeds are. Ask: *What do you think the seeds will look like? Will it be one big seed or lots of little seeds? Why do you think this?* Slice the fruit to display the seeds. Ask the students to collect at least three seeds from the display that are as different as possible, and to stick them on PCM B7. They should write where each seed came from, and describe some similarities and differences between the seeds, such as size, shape, colour and texture.

2 Give each group a set of young bean seedlings at various stages of growth. Tell the students how many days it is since each seed started to grow.

Show them how to take the plant out of the pot and carefully wash the soil from the roots, then lay the plant on a paper towel. Let them use hand lenses to examine the leaves, stem and roots of the plant. Tell them to count the leaves, then cut a piece of string to match the size of the root and shoot. They should stick their pieces of string, in order of growth of the plant they represent, onto a piece of paper. If seedlings at different stages are not available, use the pictures on Slideshow 7.

3 Give each student a copy of PCM B8 and let them follow the instructions to make a 'plant head'. Tell students they are going to do a class investigation to find out what seeds need to grow well. Ask: *Do they need water? What else do they need?* They will compare their plants to some plants kept in varied conditions in the next lesson. Ask the students to predict what they think their plant heads will look like after one week and to draw a picture on Workbook page 16.

Consolidate and review

- Explain that seeds produce new plants and are also an important source of food for animals and humans. Create a class list of all the seeds that we can eat.

Differentiation

■ All of the students should be able to describe differences between the seeds they have chosen, such as shape and colour. Some may describe differences in less obvious features, such as texture.

● Most of the students should be able to work collaboratively to arrange the lengths of string in the correct order with little support. Some may like to measure with a ruler, and this should be encouraged.

▲ Some of the students should be able to follow instructions to make their plant head and make predictions about how it will grow, but may need help to show this pictorially. If the students struggle to independently complete the sentences about what the plant will need to grow, remind them about what they have learned in the lesson.

1.11 From seeds to plants

Student's Book pages 22–23

Biology learning objective

- Explore how seeds grow into flowering plants.

Resources

- Workbook page 17
- Video B7: Seed to plant
- PCM B9: Lemon tree life cycle (1)
- PCM B10: Lemon tree life cycle (2)
- DVD Activity B3: Tomato plant life cycle

Classroom equipment

- selection of fruit, knife, plate
- pictures of tree saplings, or real ones in pots if possible
- scissors and glue
- paper and coloured pens or pencils
- the 'plant heads' from the previous lesson

Scientific enquiry skills

- *Ideas and evidence:* Try to answer questions by collecting evidence through observation.

Key words

- fruit
- seed
- life cycle
- flower
- adult

⚠ Some of the students may have a nut allergy. All of the students should wear plastic gloves if touching nuts. Remind the students to wash their hands after handling the seedlings. Check that no seeds that are used are poisonous. Warn students not to eat any of the seeds or fruit, and to wash their hands after handling them. Supervise students when they are using scissors and glue.

Scientific background

The plant *life cycle* describes the process through which a plant passes. Every plant goes through its own life cycle. The cycle starts with the *seed*. Seeds are produced by *adult plants* and usually develop inside *fruits*, which are formed from the *flowers* of the plant. The seed germinates (starts to grow) and becomes a seedling, which grows to break through the soil. The seedling absorbs sunlight and water to grow. The seedling grows into a mature plant and then moves into the flowering stage in which it makes seeds. When new seeds fall to the ground, the plant life cycle begins again. The cycle is continuous, with every plant producing seeds that will germinate into new plants. Note that at this stage, students learn about the life cycles of flowering plants and those that produce fruit. Not all types of plants do this, and this will be taught in later stages. In this lesson, the students do a class investigation into the effects of light and water on plant growth, using the 'plant heads' they made in the previous lesson as control plants.

Introduction

- Ask: *What types of fruit do you know of?* Give each group a bowl with six different common fruits in it. Encourage the students to feel the fruit and smell

them. Have a plate ready with small samples of each fruit for the students to taste. Let them also observe the seeds. Ask what they see: *What is similar and what is different? Did you see anything unusual?* Ask one person in each group to report back to the class about one named fruit. Encourage the other groups to add to the description. Highlight that some fruits are not safe to eat and warn students that they must never eat any fruit without asking an adult if it is safe first.

- Introduce the key terms: *fruit, flower, seed, adult* plant and *life cycle*. Write each word on the board and point out the spelling and pronunciation. Ask the students to repeat each word after you.

Teaching and learning activities

- Ask the students to look at the pictures on Student's Book page 22. Ask: *What changes do you see? What happens to the flower?* (It turns into a fruit.) *What can you then see on the plant?* (a fruit) Encourage the students by directing them to look at the various parts, such as the stems. Let them discuss the questions in their groups. Establish that plants change as they grow. Take feedback and discuss the students' ideas as a class. Explain that the pictures show the stages in the life cycle of a plant, in this case a tomato plant.

- Ask: *Why is there a seed inside the fruit?* Establish that the seed is part of the plant's life cycle. Remind the students that seeds grow into plants. Explain that many plants grow and form flowers. Fruit form from the flower on a plant. The fruit contain the seeds. The seeds go on to grow into new plants. Illustrate on the board how a seed turns into a fruit: seed → seedling → plant → flower → fruit

- Show the students Video B7, a time-lapse recording of a seed growing and the adult plants. Ask the students to describe what they can see at the different stages of growth, and discuss this as a class. Then look at the pictures on Student's Book page 23. Make sure students understand the questions, and work through the answers as a class.

- Ask the groups to brainstorm how trees are different from the tomato plant on Student's Book page 22. Ask: *Do trees have flowers?* (Some do.) Elicit that trees are bigger and taller, and have a woody stem called a *trunk*. At this stage, many students find it hard to accept that a tree is a plant. If you can, show the students some saplings, possibly in pots, and then a mature tree of the same species. If real saplings are not available, pictures will act as substitutes. Ask the students to say how trees change as they get older.

Graded activities

1 Give each pair of students a copy of PCM B9 and PCM B10. Ask them to cut out the pictures of the different stages of growth of a lemon tree on PCM B9 and to glue them in the correct order on PGM B10 to show the complete life cycle. Ask: *What do you know about the fruit? Does the fruit change as it grows?* Elicit that they get bigger and change colour, starting off green and turning to yellow. Emphasise that all fruits change colour as they ripen, and that this is how animals and humans know when they are ready to eat.

2 Give each student some paper and coloured pens and ask them to draw the life cycle of their favourite fruit. They can refer to their completed PCM 10 for guidance. Encourage the students to show their life cycles to the class and explain the different stages, from seed to fruit. Ask: *What is happening at each stage? Which part of the plant can we eat?*

3 Remind the students about the 'plant heads' they made in the previous lesson and what they are for: a class investigation to find out what seeds need to grow into healthy plants. Tell them that you have been looking after four different plant heads: one watered and kept in the light; one not watered and kept in the light; one watered and kept in the dark; one not watered and kept in the dark. Before you show these to the students, ask: *What do you think the plant head will look like if it has had no water? What will it look like if it has had no light?* Let them discuss these questions in groups. They should draw pictures to show their ideas and make predictions on Workbook page 17. Ask the students to look at their own plant heads. Then show your four plant heads to the class. Ask the students to observe the differences and to discuss them in groups. To finish, ask: *What do seeds need to grow into healthy plants?*

Consolidate and review

- Write these words on the board: *seedling*, *water*, *flower*, *seed*, *fruit*, *grow*. Ask the students to use them in the correct order to describe to a partner how seeds grow into adult plants.

- Let the students complete DVD Activity B3 to consolidate their learning.

Differentiation

■ All of the students should be able to talk and work together to put the pictures in the correct order to show the life cycle of a lemon tree.

● Most of the students should be able to draw the life cycle of their chosen fruit with little prompting. Some may find this easier than others. Circulate, asking questions to guide them to the correct answers.

▲ Some of the students should be able to work collaboratively, asking and answering questions to clarify their thinking. Some should be able to make predictions, but may struggle to show this pictorially. Remind the students what they have learned in the past two lessons.

Consolidation

Student's Book page 24

Biology learning objectives

- Know that plants are living things.
- Know that there are living things and things that have never been alive.
- Explore ways that different animals and plants inhabit local environments.
- Name the major parts of a plant, looking at real plants and models.
- Know that plants need light and water to grow.
- Explore how seeds grow into flowering plants.

Resources

- Workbook page 18
- Assessment Sheets B1, B2 and B3

Classroom equipment

- coloured pens or pencils

Looking back

- Use the summary points on Student's Book page 24 to review the key things that the students have learned in the topic. Ask questions such as: *What can you remember about the parts of plants?* (flowers, stem, root, leaf) *What happens when plants grow?* (They make flowers.) *What forms from the flowers?* (a fruit) *What is inside the fruit?* (seeds) *What happens to the seeds?* (They grow into new plants.)

- Distribute some coloured pens and ask the students to draw the plant of their choice on Workbook page 18. When they have completed their drawings, the students should label the parts of the plant and write where the plant lives. Encourage the students to briefly describe the type of environment that the plant lives in. Circulate, asking: *Is it hot or cold where your plant lives? Is it wet or dry?* This activity will show you how well the students have understood the topic.

How well do you remember?

You may use the revision and consolidation activities on Student's Book page 24, either as a test or as a paired class activity. If you are using the activities as a test, have the students work on their own to complete the tasks in writing, and then collect and mark the work. If you are using them as a class activity, you may prefer to let the students do the tasks orally. Circulate as they discuss the questions and observe the students carefully to see who is confident and who is unsure of the concepts.

Some suggested answers

1 Students' own answers.
2 Shady, cool, damp.

3 Answers might include: trees, mushrooms, ferns, etc.
4 They both have leaves, stem, flowers. Only the living plant can grow, move, sense, and produce fruit and seeds (breathe, eat).
5 Students' own drawings.

Assessment

A more formal assessment of the students' understanding of the topic can be undertaken using Assessment Sheets B1, B2 and B3. These can be completed in class or as a homework task.

Students following Cambridge Primary Science Framework will write progression tests set and supplied by Cambridge Assessment International Education at this level and feedback will be given regarding their achievement levels.

Assessment Sheet answers

Sheet B1

1 Students' own drawings. [3]
2 Students' own drawings. [3]
3 It can move. It can grow. [2]
4 True [1]
5 Students' own answers. [1]

Sheet B2

1 Students' labelled drawings. [5]
2 Polar bear, arctic hare, arctic fox [3]; desert [1]
3 true [1]

Sheet B3

1 2 - adult plant, 3 - flowers grow, 4 - fruit forms, 5 - seeds develop inside the fruit [4]
2 sweet potato, carrot [2]
3 bird [1], because it can fly or it only has two legs or it has feathers [1]
4 True, false [2]

Student's Book answers

Pages 2–3
1 Students' own answers.
2 Living things might include: trees, people, flowers, grass, ducks, birds, goat.
3 Non-living things might include: fence, bench, buildings, food, clothes.
4 Elephant, tree, plant, goat, butterfly.
5 Pencil, chair, bicycle, tea.

Pages 4–5
1 Living things might include: bird, animals, snake, spider, people, trees, pond plants, frogs, butterflies, duck, flamingos, tortoise.
2 Non-living things might include: fences, stones, rocks, teddy bear, clothes, water, building, lamp post.
3 Plants might include: trees, pond plants. Animals might include: zebra, giraffe, antelope, snake, spider, duck, flamingos, frogs, butterflies, bird, tortoise, people.
4 five types
5 Same: they have green leaves, they are living, they are growing. Different: some live in water, some live on land, some are large trees, some are small plants.

Pages 6–7
1 Answers might include: outside, on the window ledge, in plant pots, in the ground.
2 Yes. They are growing.
3 The pink flower will not grow even if it is watered because it is non-living.
4 If you do not water the purple plant it will not grow (it will die) because it is a living thing.

Pages 8–9
1 Non-living things might include: fire, boat, hut, stones, river, mountains, cooking pot.
2 Any of the objects made from wood were once alive (trees).
3 The stones, mountains and water have never been alive.
4 A tree can grow, sense, move, (breathe, eat) because it is living. An object made from wood is non-living and cannot do these things.

Pages 10–11
1 Picture A: hot, dry, dusty, etc. Picture B: cold, icy, etc. Picture C: wet, hot, etc. Picture D: cool, windy, etc.
2 In a cold/snowy/icy/polar environment.
3 Answers might include: polar bear, penguin. Penguins huddle together. Polar bears have thick fur.
4 Answers might include: sea weed (under water), pond lilies (on top of water).

Pages 12–13
1 Picture A: hot, wet, etc. Picture C: hot, dry, etc.
2 Cactus: fleshy stem that holds water, thin needle-like leaves; Rainforest plants: tall stems, big leaves.

3 Answers might include: insects, spiders, birds, frogs, monkeys/apes, snakes.
4 Short/low to the ground. Growing in between the rocks so will have shallow roots. The flowers are yellow and the leaves are small.
5 The plants grow low to the ground to avoid the wind, etc.

Pages 14–15
1 Picture A: small plants growing on the rocks, water, shade. Picture B: tree stumps, rotten wood, small mosses growing on the old wood, dead leaves, shady damp places.
2 Both environments have small plants, shade, etc.
3 Small animals such as: woodlice, ants, spiders, worms, slugs, snails, centipedes, frogs, toads.

Pages 16–17
1 They both have roots, green leaves, a stem and flowers. Only plant B has fruit.
2 Yes.
3 No.
4 Answers might include: yam, cassava, potato, carrot, swede, radish, mooli.
5 Answers might include: the leaves of lettuces/cabbages, the seeds of fennel/coconut/sunflower.

Pages 18–19
1 They all have leaves and a stem. Only plant C has fruit. Plants A and B are not healthy.
2 The unhealthy plants have not had enough water or light.
3 It is too hot and there is not enough water for the plants to grow well.

Pages 20–21
1 Avocado: one big, round seed. Tomatoes: lots of small seeds. Peanuts: 2-3 round seeds in each shell. Dates: one hard, long seed.
2 A coconut is a seed. It is the part of the plant that will grow into a new plant.
3 To grow more plants of the same kind.
4 The stem grows taller and thicker. The leaves grow bigger and there are more of them.
5 The children are planting some seeds.

Pages 22–23
1 The pictures are showing the life cycle of a plant.
2 Plants need warmth, soil, air (space), water and nutrients to grow.
3 The plant gets taller, the stem grows, it has more leaves, the flowers grow, the fruit grows.
4 4, 2, 3, 5, 1

2.1 **We are similar**

Student's Book pages 26–27

Biology learning objective

- Recognise the similarities and differences between each other.

Resources

- PCM B11: My family

Classroom equipment

- old magazines
- scissors
- paper
- colouring pens or pencils

- students' photographs from home of themselves and of a family member
- large sheets of card

Scientific enquiry skills

- *Ideas and evidence:* Try to answer questions by collecting evidence through observation.

Key words

- **human**   • **similar**   • **feature**

 Supervise the students when they use scissors.

Scientific background

All human beings have some similar features. People have the same general sort of shape, same body parts and same facial features, but the appearance of these and characteristics such as height, weight and hair colour vary from person to person. During reproduction, parents pass on genetic material to their children. However, not all the characteristics a parent can offer are passed on. Therefore, children inherit features from both parents. These features are called *hereditary characteristics*, and include things such as hair and eye colour and whether the tongue can be rolled or not. Some characteristics such as scars are acquired during a lifetime rather than inherited. Because of genetics, people within a family can bear a very strong likeness to each other. However, even people from very different ethnic groups have recognisable features that are the same. In this unit, the students will focus on similar features that people share. Differences between people will be covered in Unit 2.2.

Introduction

- Use the topic opener photograph on Student's Book page 25 as a talking point. Ask the students to describe what they can see. Ask them: *What do you think this topic will be about?* Let them briefly discuss this in groups. Tell them that they are going to learn more about humans.

- Ask the class to look at the picture at the bottom of Student's Book page 26. Ask: *What can you see in*

the picture? Take feedback and guide the students to establish that the photo shows an extended family: three generations of the same family. Ask: *Can you see any things that are the same?* Elicit that people in a family often have some things in common.

- Introduce the key words: *human, similar, feature*. Write them on the board and point out how each word is spelled and pronounced. Ask the students to repeat the words after you. Explain that we use the term 'similar features' to describe things that look the same between different people. Ask the students to think of a similar feature that they have in common with someone else. For example, ask: *Do you have brown hair? Who else has brown hair?* Introduce new words as necessary.

Teaching and learning activities

- Ask the students to brainstorm some similarities between humans. Remind them to think about people from different countries around the world, not just the people they know personally. Allow them time to discuss their ideas in groups. Then take feedback and compile a class list on the board.

- Encourage the students to bring into school a photograph of themselves. Mix up the photographs and ask one student to pick and look at one photo (make sure no one sees which picture they have selected). They must describe the student in the photograph without using their name. The other members of the class should guess who it is from the description. Be sensitive to the students in your class to avoid embarrassing any of them. Shuffle the photographs again and repeat for another member of the class. When a number of rounds have been played, the students will be familiar with the process of describing someone using fine detail. The students can use this skill in the graded activities which follow.

● Have the students work in pairs to draw each other and colour their pictures. Ask them to discuss how they are similar and how they are different. (Differences between humans will be covered in the next unit.) Take feedback, encouraging the students to use a wide range of adjectives, e.g. *tall*, *short*, *brown*, *blue*, etc. and comparatives, e.g. *bigger*, *smaller*. If some students need support, you could write a list of suitable words on the board to give them ideas.

● Make sure the students understand the question on Student's Book page 27. Ask them to find and name the features that the children have in common. Let them discuss their answer in groups. If the students need some guidance, refer them to the class lists on the board. This activity will reinforce the idea that, although people come from many different countries and cultures around the world, they all have some features in common.

Graded activities

1 The students should collect as many pictures of different people as possible. These can be real family photos or cut from magazines that you bring to class. Ask groups of students to sort a selection of pictures according to their own criteria. They should then explain their reasons to the rest of the class. Ask: *Why did you sort the photos in this way? What features do each group have in common?* The criteria could include age, hair colour, height, etc. The choice of criteria is not important, but students should correctly sort the pictures so that all photos in a given group fulfil the chosen criteria.

2 Give each student a copy of PCM B11. Ask them to think about members of their family and the similar features that they share with them. They should draw pictures and write the names of the family members on PCM B11. Circulate, offering support by asking: *Which things are the same? Are your ears similar? Do you have the same colour eyes?*

3 Tell the students that they are going to do a short presentation about someone in their family. Ask the students to bring into school a photograph of a family member. Ideally they should share some similar features. Allow the students time to prepare. Circulate, offering support and encouragement. Remind the students to describe the family member in as much detail as possible and to point out the features which they have in common with them. Then divide the class into groups and ask each student to give their presentation to the rest of their group.

Consolidate and review

● Give each student their photograph, mounted on a large sheet of card. Ask the students to make a poster about themselves. They should write their name, their age and some words to describe their appearance.

● Ask the students to make up a short story about their chosen family member from the activity. Let them tell their story to classmates in their group.

Differentiation

■ All of the students should be able to identify some similar features between people and correctly sort the pictures into groups based on criteria of their choice. Most of the students should be able to explain the reasoning for their chosen criteria with some support.

● Most of the students should be able to draw pictures of family members and describe some similar features. Some may find the descriptions harder than others. Circulate, offering support and asking questions to guide their thinking.

▲ Some of the students should be able to give a detailed description of shared features with a family member of their choice. Some may be able to do this independently, others may need more help. If so, you could write a frame on the board to provide a structure for their presentation.

2.2 We are different

Student's Book pages 28–29

Biology learning objective

- Recognise the similarities and differences between each other.

Resources

- Workbook page 19
- PCM B12: Picture of my friend
- PCM B13: Spot the differences
- Slideshow B8: What can you do?

Classroom equipment

- rulers, squared paper
- paper, washable stamp pads or non-toxic paint, sponges, magnifying hand lenses

Scientific enquiry skills

- *Plan investigative work:* Make predictions.
- *Obtain and present evidence:* Explore and observe in order to collect evidence (measurements and observations) to answer questions.
- *Consider evidence and approach:* Make comparisons; compare what happened with predictions.

Key words

- **different**
- **unique**

> ⚠ The students must thoroughly wash their hands after making their fingerprints.

Scientific background

All living things vary in many ways; in fact, no two are alike. Even identical twins are different in certain ways. Humans all have the same general sort of shape, but their height, weight, face shape, etc. are all different.

Growth of the young human body takes place continuously, although the process takes place so slowly that we do not usually notice the changes. Some children grow faster than others, though all children grow through periods of differing growth rate. As we grow, all parts of our body grow bigger until we reach adulthood. At this point most growth stops, apart from hair and nails. Various measurements can be used to measure human growth accurately. These include height, hand span and foot size. Weight is not a good measurement to use, as it is greatly affected by what and how much we eat. As we grow, our bodies change and we learn new skills. Children learn to do things for themselves as they grow up and develop.

Introduction

- Explain that all people have the same sort of bodies, with head, arms and legs, but that they also have many things which are different, such as height, hair colour, eye colour, etc. Ask the class to look at the top picture on Student's Book page 28. Ask: *In what ways are the children the same? In what ways are they different?*

- Introduce the key words for this unit: *unique* and *different*. Write the words on the board and point out how each one is spelled and pronounced.

- Say: *We may have some features in common, but we also have differences.* Explain to the class that everyone's fingerprints are different. Give each group a washable stamp pad or non-toxic paint, a sponge and paper, to make fingerprints. Let them examine each other's fingerprints to check that they are different. Provide magnifying hand lenses so they can look closely. Ask: *What other things about people are different?* Take feedback.

Teaching and learning activities

- Ask the students to discuss some of the ways the body changes as it grows. Use these prompts: *Say how your body changes as you grow. Will you keep growing forever?* Make a list of the ways in which humans change as they get older.

- Ask the students to discuss how they know that they have grown. They should be aware they have grown when clothes no longer fit, or when their hair or fingernails need cutting. Discuss how we can measure the growth of a child and how different parts of the body change as we grow. Ask: *What parts of your body could you use to measure how you grow over a period of time?* Take feedback and discuss their ideas. Tell the students that height is not the only feature that shows growth.

Mark a line along the ground, about 1.5 metres long. Show the students how to measure it in 'foot lengths', starting with the heel of one foot at one end, then placing the heel of the other foot immediately in front of the first foot. Provide a similar line for each group. Let them count and record how many 'steps' each student takes, to reach the end of the line. Ask them to compare their results.

Ask the students if they think that the older students in the class are the tallest. Take a class vote on it and record what the students think. Ask the students to line up. Arrange them into height order, from tallest to shortest. Next, ask the students to form another line, but this time in age order, from oldest to youngest. Ask: *Are you standing in the same place as before?* Ask the students if their predictions were correct. It is unlikely that you will find a pattern of oldest to youngest giving a direct correlation to height. This is a good point for discussion, and the students should try to explain why a pattern was not necessarily found. Ask: *Why was the tallest child not the oldest?* (Because children grow at different rates.)

Make sure students understand the questions on Student's Book page 29. Let them discuss their answers in groups. Then take feedback as a class.

Graded activities

1 Ask the students to work in pairs. Give each student a copy of PCM B12. Explain that they need to draw a picture and describe their partner's features. Once the students have completed the activity, ask them to say how they are different from each other. The rest of the class can comment on whether they agree or not.

2 Discuss the different things that people can do at different ages. Ask: *What can you do now that you could not do when you were a toddler?* Show the class Slideshow B8. Ask: *What can you do now that you could not do when you could only crawl? What can you do that a grandparent cannot? What can an elder brother or sister do that you are not allowed to do?*

3 Tell the students that they are going to investigate and compare the size of their hand spans. *Ask: Do you think that the oldest student in the class will have the biggest hand span?* As a class, discuss how to take fair measurements. Ask: *Where on*

the hand are you going to measure the hand span? What will you use to measure? Less able students may prefer to draw around their hands on squared paper and compare the drawings. More able students should be able to measure using a ruler. Ask students to complete the activity on Workbook page 19. Discuss their findings as a class. Ask whether their predictions were correct and for them to try to explain why.

Consolidate and review

Give each student a copy of PCM B13. Ask them to look at the two faces and to find and circle the five differences.

Ask questions to encourage a class discussion: *Who is the tallest person in the class? Did they have the biggest hand span? What do you think affects how fast we grow?* (age, health and diet)

Differentiation

■ All of the students should be able to draw a reasonable picture of their partner from first-hand observations, describe features and suggest a range of differences when comparing.

● Most of the students should be able to work in groups to share ideas when identifying different abilities at different stages of growth and development. More able students may start to describe physical characteristics as a way of explaining the differences.

▲ Some of the students should be able to make predictions and then follow instructions to take accurate measurements. Some may need more help than others. Circulate, offering help with completing the practical element if necessary and then asking questions to lead their thinking when comparing their results.

2.3 **Parts of the body**

Student's Book pages 30–31

Biology learning objective
- Recognise and name the main external parts of the body.

Resources
- Workbook page 20
- PCM B14: Where do you wear it?
- Video B8: Children playing
- DVD Activity B4: My body

Classroom equipment
- two balls
- lining paper or wallpaper
- coloured pens or pencils
- scraps of fabric

- glue
- recorded music that can be easily stopped and re-started

Scientific enquiry skills
- *Ideas and evidence:* Try to answer questions by collecting evidence through observation.

Key words
- **body**

⚠ Supervise the students when they use glue. Make sure that the students take care not to jostle other students or bump into classroom furniture when they are performing movement-based activities.

Scientific background

The human body is made up of a head, a neck, a torso, two arms and two legs. The human body is designed to stand erect, to walk on two feet and to use the arms to carry and lift. The head has two eyes that allow us to see, two ears that allow us to hear, a nose that lets us smell and a mouth for eating and speaking. (Students will learn about sense organs and their five senses in Unit 2.7.) We also have hair to protect our scalp and eyebrows, and eyelashes to protect our eyes. The torso contains the majority of the body's organs, including the heart and lungs, which are located in the chest, and the digestive organs which are located in the abdomen. The arms are joined to the torso by the shoulders, and there is a hand on each arm. Each hand has four fingers and an opposable thumb, so we are able to grasp things. The legs are joined to the torso at the hips. There is a foot on each leg, and ten toes on each foot. All of the limbs are jointed, to allow flexibility and movement. At this stage, the students need to know the main external parts of the body.

Introduction

- Say that you are going to draw something on the board and the students have to guess what it is. Draw a body, bit by bit, on the board. Direct the students to Student's Book page 30. Discuss the picture and questions as a class. Ask: *Who knows*

what the parts of our body are called? Can you point to them on your own body? Introduce the key word *body* and also the words for the body parts that are labelled in the picture: *head, shoulder, neck, arm, hand, finger, chest, stomach, foot, leg, toe.* Label the body you have drawn on the board. Tell the class that they are going to learn more about their bodies.

- Make sure that the students all understand that these body parts are common to them all, and that although they may be of different sizes (e.g. leg length), they all serve the same function. Be sensitive when talking about the body parts in case not all children have all parts. Ask: *How many legs do you have? How many fingers do you have?*

- The students will have played body part games during their early years education. This orientation exercise gives the students something familiar to build on and will help increase their vocabulary. Play 'Simon says' with the class. If you say: *Simon says...* they must do the action that you say next. If you do not start with: *Simon says...* they should not do the action. Tell students to listen carefully and follow directions. Start with: *Simon says, put your finger on your head.* Give support by pointing to your head and putting your finger on it. Try: *Put your hand on your chest.* The students should ignore this.

Teaching and learning activities

- Ask the students to discuss, in their groups, all the things they can do. Say that you are going to make a class list on the board. Take feedback from the groups. Ask them to start their responses with: *I can...* Take an idea from each group, in turn, until they have no more suggestions.

- Stand in front of the students and hold up your hands. Indicate your feet, asking: *Why do we have hands and feet? What can they help us to do?* Arrange the students in two groups, each forming a large circle. Include an adult in each circle. Explain that the adult will name someone in the circle and then throw a ball to them. That student must try to catch the ball. Then they name another student, and throw the ball to that student, and so on. Ask: *What parts of your body are you using to do this?* (arms, hands) Repeat, this time gently kicking the ball. Ask: *What parts of the body are you using now?* (legs, feet)

- Make sure students understand the questions on Student's Book page 31. Let them discuss their answers in groups. Then take feedback as a class.

- Pin a long sheet of paper to a wall and ask a student to stand in front of it. Use a marker pen to draw round the outline of the student, to give a body outline. Repeat for each group. Pin each group's body outline to the wall and let the students add features to the face. Let them use fabric scraps to add clothes. Ask each group to add the labels at the correct places on the body outlines. Many at this stage will need help with the labelling but the discussion of what the parts are is at least as important as whether they spell the words correctly.

Graded activities

1 Give each student a copy of PCM B14, which shows various items of clothing. Explain that they need to match each item of clothing to the body part that it is worn on. Students can work in pairs to do this. Circulate to check that they are matching correctly, asking questions to guide them as necessary. Once they have completed the activity, encourage them to discuss their experiences of wearing similar items of clothing.

2 Show the class Video B8, of some children playing. Ask: *What is happening? What parts of their bodies are the children using?* Let the students discuss this in groups, encouraging

them to ask questions, share ideas and challenge the ideas of others. Take feedback and discuss answers as a class. Summarise by eliciting that the children are using all parts of their bodies.

3 Tell the students that you would like them to draw a picture of themselves on Workbook page 20. They should then label the different body parts. Circulate to check that they are adding the labels in the correct places. Ask questions such as: *Where is your arm? What is at the end of your arm? Can you find this on your drawing?* This activity should show you how well the students have understood the unit.

Consolidate and review

- Tell the students that they are going to play 'Musical statues.' Explain that when the music is playing they can move about and play. As soon as the music stops, the students must 'freeze', standing still, just like a statue. If a student moves, say: *I saw you moving your arm/leg/head, you are out of the game.*

- Let the students discuss what they know about hands and what they can do with them. Ask them to demonstrate, for example, wiggling their fingers.

- Let the students complete DVD Activity B4 to consolidate their learning.

Differentiation

■ All of the students should be able to match the clothing to the correct body parts. Even if some of the clothing is unfamiliar to the students, they should still be able to match correctly using the size and shape of the clothing.

● Most of the students should be able to talk and work together to share ideas and identify the different body parts. More able students may discuss that different body parts can do different things.

▲ Some of the students should be able to draw an accurate representation of themselves and correctly label the different body parts. Some may struggle with the labelling. If so, offer support and guidance to guide them to the correct answers.

Big Cat 🐾

Students who read *Big Cat The robot* will quickly realise how important it is that everyone, even a robot, needs a head!

2.4 Healthy and unhealthy foods

Student's Book pages 32–33

Biology learning objective

- Know about the need for a healthy diet, including the right types of food and water.

Resources

- Workbook page 21
- Slideshow B9: Different foods

Classroom equipment

- large sheets of paper
- pictures of different foods and drinks
- two different colours of sticky notes
- research materials

Scientific enquiry skills

- *Ideas and evidence:* Try to answer questions by collecting evidence through observation.
- *Consider evidence and approach:* Model and communicate ideas in order to share, explain and develop them.

Key words

- diet
- healthy
- unhealthy

 If the students use the internet, ensure they do so safely and always under adult supervision.

Scientific background

The food we eat on a regular basis is called our *diet*. Many people now have access to a wide range of foods from around the world, which helps provide an interesting and varied diet. Humans and animals need food for energy, to grow and to stay healthy. Animals cannot make their own food and need to eat plants and other animals to survive. Every animal has a particular diet that it needs in order to stay healthy, including humans. It is important that we eat a variety of different food types and that we eat the right amount of each type of food.

Foods are split into different groups for classification purposes. Each food group has a different function. Carbohydrates are sugary and starchy foods which provide the body with 'fuel' for energy. Protein foods such as meat and fish provide body-building chemicals for growing muscles, hair, nails, skin and organs. Other nutrients are also important for a well-balanced diet, including minerals and vitamins. The concept of a varied diet is not introduced until Stage 3 of this course. At Stage 1 the students do not need to understand the different food groups, but they should recognise a variety of examples of healthy foods (such as fruit, vegetables, bread, rice, fish and eggs) and unhealthy foods (those high in sugar, salt and fat). They should also know that we should eat plenty of healthy foods, ideally on a daily basis, and we should eat fewer unhealthy foods.

Introduction

- Discuss with the students the fact that all living things need food and that we need to eat to stay alive. Ask: *What does it feel like when you haven't eaten for several hours? What are your favourite foods?* Compile a class list on the board of some of the students' favourite foods.

- Ask the students to look at the pictures on Student's Book pages 32–33. Allow them to discuss the questions in groups, then take feedback as a class. Explain that a wide variety of foods exist, some they will be familiar with and others not. Tell the students that they are now going to learn about healthy and unhealthy foods.

Teaching and learning activities

- Draw two plates on the board: one with a healthy meal of meat, vegetables and rice, and the other with a less healthy meal of pizza and chips. Ask the students to vote on which one is healthier and better for them. You can invite them to give reasons for their choice but do not correct any misconceptions at this stage.

- Show the class Slideshow B9 of different food types. After each picture, ask the students to name the food and ask for a show of hands if they have ever eaten that food before. Ask: *What can you tell me about the food?* Prompt the students to say whether the food comes from a plant or an animal. Write their answers on the board.

- Arrange a display of pictures of different foods. Give each student two sticky notes, of two different colours. Assign one colour to the food they like best and the other to the food they like least. Let them vote for their favourite and least favourite foods, by attaching sticky notes to the pictures. Ask them to say why they do or do not like the foods, based on how they taste or smell. Add the 'most favourite' foods to the list on the board.

- Show the class some pictures of various types of foods and drinks. Ask the students to sort them into groups according to their own criteria. Many students will sort the foods into those that they like and those that they do not, or choose colour as a simple criterion. Discuss with the students why they have grouped their foods in a certain way. The types of foods should be discussed in terms of meat, fish, cheese, fruit and vegetables. The correct terms, such as protein, are not needed at this stage. If they did not already, students should then re-sort the pictures into the different categories of food types. This is a good opportunity to introduce foods from other cultures and to discuss the dietary requirements of different groups of people.

Graded activities

1 Let the students complete the activity on Workbook page 21. They should circle all the healthy foods and drinks. Some students may need help distinguishing between the two. Circulate, asking questions to guide them as necessary, e.g. ask: *Do you think it is healthy? Is it good for you? Is it something we should eat a lot of?* When the students have completed the activity, ask them to name some more healthy foods and drinks.

2 Students are to do a survey of the most popular foods in the class. Ask the students to identify their favourite foods. This can be simple (favourite crisp flavour or snack food), or more complicated (favourite type of meal, e.g. roast dinner, curry, breakfast). The survey must be handled in a sensitive way to take into account the views of vegetarians and groups of people with special (often religious) beliefs about food. The data should be presented in a table or a simple graph. Remind the class that these are effective methods of recording and displaying data. Students can then use this to work in groups to make a poster of their findings. Discuss the data as a class. Help

the students to draw out any patterns in the data. More able students may wish to extend the survey to other classes. This activity provides an excellent opportunity to introduce simple spreadsheets and to use ICT skills for data collection.

3 Explain that a person's diet often depends on the part of the world that they live in and that is often based on the types of food that are available locally. Ask the students if they know where some popular international foods come from. Then ask the students to describe some foods they have tried from countries other than their own. Next, ask the students to choose a country that they would like to find more about the diet of. Working in groups, help them to do some research using reference books or the internet. Students should make a fact sheet to illustrate their findings. Display these on the wall in the classroom and discuss.

Consolidate and review

- Make a poster about healthy foods, showing fruit and vegetables, some sources of protein, e.g. chicken and cheese, a glass of water, some fibre, e.g. breakfast cereal. Display the poster in the classroom and review it at the end of the next unit to see if the students have changed their minds about what constitutes healthy eating.

- Discuss some different types of farm: dairy, poultry, vegetable, wheat, fruit orchards and animal farms.

Differentiation

■ All of the students should be able to correctly identify the healthy foods and drinks. If not, help the students by reminding them of some of the criteria for healthy foods.

● Most of the students should be able to collect some simple data and present it in either tabular or graph form with some support. Most of them should be able to share their ideas and listen to discussions to help them complete the poster of their findings.

▲ Some of the students should be able to work collaboratively, thinking critically and asking sensible questions to extend their knowledge and produce an informative fact sheet. Some students may not be working at this level yet. If so, you may prefer to do this as a more structured activity by offering a frame for them to work to.

2.5 Eating well

Scientific background

Food provides the chemicals we need to make new cells for growth, fuel for energy and helps to protect from illnesses. A healthy diet contains the different nutrients in the correct amounts to keep us healthy. Foods are split into different groups for classification purposes. Each food group has a different function. Carbohydrates are sugary and starchy foods which provide the body with 'fuel' for energy. Protein foods such as meat and fish provide body-building chemicals for growing muscles, hair, nails, skin and organs. Other nutrients are also important for a well-balanced diet, including minerals and vitamins. Some unsaturated fat helps to improve cholesterol levels and prevent health risks. It is needed for the proper functioning of the body. However, saturated fat raises the level of cholesterol in the blood, which can lead to heart disease, liver problems and obesity. Obesity is a recognised disease and is a growing problem in many countries around the world. Foods in the different food groups contain different amounts of energy. If we do not use all of the energy in our food, it turns to fat in our bodies. The amount of energy we need from our food depends on our age, our height and how much exercise we do. It is important to balance the amount of food we eat with who we are and what we do.

The concept of a varied diet is not introduced until Stage 3 of this course. At Stage 1 the students do not need to understand the different food groups, but they should appreciate the importance of eating healthy food in order for us to grow and be healthy. They should also begin to understand that there can be consequences from eating too much unhealthy food, such as weight gain and poor health.

Introduction

● Ask the students to look at the picture on Student's Book page 34. Allow them to discuss the questions in groups, then take feedback as a class. Elicit a variety of healthy food items, such as fruit, vegetables, fish, eggs, noodles, etc. Establish that we need to eat food every day but that there are many different varieties to choose from so it is possible, and preferable, to eat plenty of healthy foods.

● Explain that we need food for our bodies to work, to grow and for us to stay healthy. For this to happen, we must eat healthy food. Ask the students: *What would happen if you did not eat or drink for a couple of days?* Allow them to discuss this in groups and then gather their ideas. The students should be able to see that food is essential for life.

Teaching and learning activities

● Give each student a copy of PCM B15 and scissors. Ask them to colour the pictures and then cut out both sets of cards. Tell students that they are now going to play a game. Explain how the game of food match works: students need to match each picture card to the correct word card. Let them work in pairs to do this.

● Ask the students to sort the food picture cards from PCM B15 into groups according to their own criteria. Some students may sort the foods into those that they like and those that they do not. Others will begin to think of them in terms of how healthy they are or in basic food groups. Discuss with the students why they have grouped their foods in a certain way. This is a good opportunity to recap foods from other cultures.

● Remind students that we only need to eat certain types of foods in small amounts. Ask: *Why should we not eat too much sugary food? Why should we not eat too much fatty food?* Take suggestions from the class. Explain that we can become overweight and unhealthy.

● Ask the students to look at the pictures on Student's Book page 35. Allow them to discuss the questions in groups, then take feedback as a class.

Graded activities

1 Give each pair of students some old magazines and scissors. Ask them to cut out as many pictures of different foods as they can and then to sort the pictures into two groups: *healthy* and *unhealthy*. The pictures may be of single food items, several combined together, e.g. a sandwich, or complete meals. Once the sorting is done, ask the students to give reasons for why they have sorted the foods into each category. Ask: *Was it difficult to decide which group to put some of the food in?* This could lead to a discussion about some meals containing a mixture of healthy and unhealthy foods.

2 Ask the students to think about their favourite healthy meal and to draw a picture of it on Workbook page 22. They should then label the picture, in their own language or in English. Depending on ability, some students may add one label for the complete meal or more able students may label the individual food items. When they have completed their drawings, let the students discuss the favourite healthy meals in groups. Take feedback as a class and establish the most popular healthy meals. Stress the importance of fruit and vegetables, foods such as rice, pasta and potatoes (carbohydrates), milk and cheese (dairy), and fish and meat (proteins). (At this stage, students do not need to know the food categories shown in parentheses, only examples of healthy foods.)

3 Ask the students to name some different healthy foods. They should think of individual foods, such as meat, fish, bread, carrots, etc. rather than complete meals or food groups, e.g. vegetables. Compile a class list on the board. Elicit as wide a variety of food items as possible. Once you have created an extensive list, give each student a copy of PCM B16. Tell the students that they need to work in groups to design a healthy menu for a week at school. They can use the list on the board to give them ideas and add any others that they can think of. Once they have completed their menus, invite each group to present their menu to the class. You could then take a class vote on the best overall menu or best individual days.

Consolidate and review

● Tell students to pretend that they are going to live on a desert island for a week. There is no food on the island and no shops. They need to take everything they need with them. In groups, the students should decide what food and drink they would like to take.

Differentiation

■ All of the students should be able to identify the healthy and unhealthy foods and correctly sort them into two groups. Circulate and explain any of the food items which may be unfamiliar to the students.

● Most of the students should be able to draw an accurate picture of their chosen meal and add labels with little help, either labelling the meal as a whole or the individual elements.

▲ Some of the students should be able to work together to share ideas and think critically to design a menu which incorporates a range of healthy foods. Some may struggle to create a number of different meals. If so, remind them to look at the class list on the board and make suggestions for how different foods can be combined to make a meal. Ask questions to guide their thinking.

Students who read *Big Cat We like fruit* will recognise the different types of fruit shown in this book.

2.6 Clean water is important

Student's Book pages 36–37

Biology learning objective

- Know about the need for a healthy diet, including the right types of food and water.

Resources

- Workbook pages 23 and 24
- PCM B17: Spot the differences
- PCM B18: Wasting water
- PCM B19: Filtering water

Classroom equipment

- bottles or cups of clean water
- bottles of dirty water (water mixed with mud, leaves, twigs, etc.)
- 2-litre plastic bottle, scissors, cotton fabric, elastic band or string, cotton wool, washed gravel, washed sand, supply of dirty water (water mixed with mud, leaves, twigs, etc.)
- large tray to catch any spills from the investigation

Scientific enquiry skills

- *Plan investigative work:* Ask questions and contribute to discussions about how to seek answers; make predictions.
- *Obtain and present evidence:* Explore and observe in order to collect evidence (measurements and observations) to answer questions.
- *Consider evidence and approach:* Compare what happened with predictions.

Key words

- **water**
- **source**

⚠ Do not let the students drink any of the water that they handle. It is important that the students understand that the water you filter in the experiment will be clean, but that it will not be safe to drink. Mop up any spills immediately.

Scientific background

Humans need to drink water to stay alive, for their bodies to function well and to be healthy. Water from most sources must be cleaned before we can drink it. Clean water is safe to drink but dirty water can make humans and animals ill, and in extreme cases can even lead to death. Fresh water comes from a wide variety of sources such as rivers, lakes and wells, as well as taps and bottles. The water from taps and bottles is usually clean as it will have been processed before it reaches us. Water from wells comes largely from rainwater that has been filtered through the layers of rock to form groundwater. Because it has been filtered, it is relatively clean, but it may need to be disinfected before drinking.

As well as needing water to drink, we also use it for many other things, such as washing and cooking. Fresh water is very important in every person's life and is a precious resource, particularly in arid environments. Therefore, we must not waste it. Although about 70% of the Earth is covered in water, the vast majority of this is seawater. Seawater has salt in it and so is not good for humans and animals to drink.

Many substances are porous enough to allow water to pass through. If the pores are too large, the water will not be adequately filtered. If they are too small, they may soon block up and not allow any more water to pass through. The students do not need to know this level of detail at this stage, but the class investigation will introduce them to the idea of filtering and how well substances can filter out different types of 'dirt'.

Introduction

- Ask the students to look at the pictures on Student's Book page 36. Ask: *What is the boy doing? Why do we need to drink water?* Allow them to discuss the picture and question in groups. Take feedback as a class and elicit that all living things need water to stay alive and be healthy.

- Give each pair of students a bottle or cup containing some clean water, and another containing some dirty water. Let them examine both. Say: *Which one would you drink if you were thirsty?* Establish that it would be the clean water. Ask the students to give reasons for their choice.

- Write the key words *source* and *water* on the board and point out how each word is spelled and pronounced. Introduce the terms *clean water*, *fresh water* and *seawater* and make sure the students understand what they mean. Say they are going to learn about the importance of clean water.

Teaching and learning activities

- Explain that water from most sources must be cleaned before it is used because it contains impurities that can make you ill. Explain that there is a difference between fresh drinking water and the water in the sea, which is salty and not good to drink.

- Make sure students understand the questions on Student's Book pages 36–37. Discuss the answers as a class. Point out the picture of the well and make sure that the students know what it is and how it is used. Give each student a copy of PCM B17 and ask them to find and circle the five differences.

- Ask if they can name any other places where we can get water. If no one mentions it, suggest a river. Get the children to look at their bottles of dirty water again. Say: *The dirty water in your bottle is like the muddy water that comes from a river. Imagine that the shops have sold out of clean water. What can you do to clean your muddy water and make it safe to drink?* Tell students they are going to investigate a way of cleaning the muddy water.

- Ask: *What do you use water for?* Write a list on the board. Establish the importance of water in our lives and stress that we should view it as a precious resource and not to be wasted. Ask: *What can we do to use less water?* Allow the students time to discuss this in groups. Then give each student a copy of PCM B18 and ask them to circle all the places where water is being wasted. Discuss how the students might use less water.

Graded activities

1 Let the students complete the activity on Workbook page 23. They should tick the sources of water which are safe to drink. Circulate, asking questions to guide their thinking: *Do you think the water in the river is clean? If it is not clean, is it safe to drink?*

2 Ask the students to think about how they use water at home. Remind them to think about all the different rooms and also any areas outside, such as a garden or balcony. Encourage the students to think of some less obvious examples, such as a washing machine or watering indoor plants.

Ask them to write or draw pictures on Workbook page 24. Offer help as necessary. Ask: *Does watering the plants use more or less water than having a shower?* This will encourage them to think about how much water is used for everyday tasks.

3 Demonstrate the filtration experiment to the class. (Detailed instructions are given on PCM B19.) Ask the students to predict what they think will happen when you pour the dirty water through the filter. Write their prediction on the board. Pour a glass of dirty water through the filter. Ask: *What can you observe? Does the water look cleaner?* Allow them to discuss this in groups and then take feedback as a class. Ask: *What happened? Was your prediction correct?* Explain in very simple terms that the different substances help to take out different things from the dirty water. Make sure the students understand that even though the water they are filtering and collecting from the model well looks clean, it is not safe to drink. To turn it into safe drinking water, chemicals would need to be added to kill any germs or bacteria.

Consolidate and review

- Give the students a selection of different sized and shaped containers and some water. Let them pour water from one to the other trying not to spill any water or have any left over.

Differentiation

■ All of the students should be able to identify which sources of water are safe to drink, demonstrating they have understood the lesson. Circulate, asking questions if the students need some guidance.

● Most of the students should be able to identify and describe some obvious uses of water in the home such as in the shower or bath. More able students may identify a wider range of uses, including some less obvious ones such as in a dishwasher.

▲ Some of the students should be able to predict the outcome of the investigation with a little help. Students should be able to work collaboratively, asking and answering questions to clarify their thinking. More able students should be able to provide reasons.

2.7 Our senses

Student's Book pages 38–39

Biology learning objective

- Explore how senses enable humans and animals to be aware of the world around them.

Resources

- Workbook pages 25 and 26
- Slideshow B10: Colours
- Audio clip B1: Animal sounds
- PCM B20: Fruity smells
- PCM B21: Senses in action

Classroom equipment

- mystery objects, a soft fabric bag
- empty drink cans, sticky tape
- rice, sand, small nails, tacks
- selection of different objects
- white sheet
- four small pots with lids
- four different fruits with a strong smell

Note: Before the lesson, prepare four small plastic pots. Label them from 1 to 4, and make some small holes in the lid of each one.

Scientific enquiry skills

- *Ideas and evidence:* Try to answer questions by collecting evidence through observation.

Key words

- **sense organ**
- **senses**

⚠️ Be aware that some students, particularly boys, may be colour-blind and have problems differentiating certain colours.

Scientific background

The human head has on it all of our *sense organs*: two *eyes* for *sight*, two *ears* for *hearing*, a *nose* for *smell*, a *tongue* for *taste* and *skin* for *touch*. The sense organs are connected by nerves to the brain, which tells us the things that our senses detect.

Although we have five senses, we rarely use them individually. For example, we use smell and taste together, and often support one sense with another, for example when looking at an object and feeling it at the same time. If we lose one of our senses, it may be that our other senses become sharper, to compensate.

Introduction

- Draw a face on the board. Point to each of the five sense organs and ask: *What is this? What do we call this part of the face?* Elicit the correct names and label the face. Address any misconceptions.
- Explain that some parts of our faces have important jobs. Ask: *What are these jobs? What do different parts of our faces do? What are our eyes, ears, nose and mouth for?* Let the students discuss their answers in small groups. Take feedback, one point from each group in turn, until all their ideas are exhausted. Discuss their ideas and explain that eyes let us see, ears let us hear, our nose lets us smell and our mouth lets us talk and eat.

- Show Slideshow B10, about colours. For each colour, ask: *What is this colour?* Indicate the name on the slide and say the colour. On the last slide, point to colours at random and ask: *What colour is this?* Concentrate on the colours that were unfamiliar to the students. Ask: *Which part of your body do you use to see the colours?* Explain that the students are using their eyes to see.

- Introduce the term *sense*. Many students will confuse the meaning with common usage, e.g. *They do not have any common sense.* Explain to them that in the context of their body the term has a very specific meaning. Introduce the five sense key words and write each one on the board next to the correct sense organ: *eye – sight, ear – hearing, nose – smell, tongue – taste, skin – touch.* Point out the spelling and pronunciation of all the words for this unit. Ask the students to repeat each word after you. Then tell the class that they are going to learn more about their senses and sense organs.

Teaching and learning activities

- Make sure students understand the questions on Student's Book pages 38 and 39. Talk about what is happening in the pictures. Ask: *What can the girl smell? Does she like the smell? Do you like the smell of flowers?* Ask: *What can the boys taste?*

Which sense are they using? Point out that we often use more than one sense at a time.

● Put equal amounts of a substance into a pair of empty drink cans. Repeat for a variety of substances, such as rice, sand, small nails, tacks, water and polystyrene packing beans to produce a set of pairs of cans. Tape the openings shut. Shuffle the cans. Ask the students to match the cans into pairs that contain the same substance by shaking them and comparing the sounds. Ask: *What made you sort the cans in this way?* Establish that they used their ears and that hearing is one of our senses.

● Show the class a soft fabric bag, with something hidden inside it. Invite individual students to feel the object, through the bag, and describe what they feel. Ask the students if the object is rough, smooth, hard or soft, and so on. Ask the students to guess what the object is. When they make a correct guess, repeat with a different object. Establish that we use our hands to feel things and our sense of touch to identify them.

● Play a game with about eight objects on a white sheet. Cover them over after about 15 seconds and ask the students to tell you what was on the sheet. This can be made progressively harder by adding more objects to demonstrate that the eye is the organ of sight and the brain has to remember what the eye has seen.

● Put a slice of fruit into each small, numbered pot. Show the group that you can smell the fruit through the holes in the lids. Then let the students smell the four pots and try to identify the fruit inside. Ask them to draw a picture of the fruit that they have identified, in the numbered spaces on PCM B20. When the students have completed the task, take feedback and see how many students guessed correctly. Ask: *Was it more difficult to identify the fruit when you could only use your sense of smell?* Stress again that we often use more than one sense at a time.

Graded activities

1 Let the students complete the activity on Workbook page 25. They should match each sense to the correct sense organ. Circulate, asking questions to guide their thinking: *Which part of our body do we use to see? When we see something, which sense are we using?*

2 Let the students complete the activity on PCM B21 in pairs. They need to identify the senses that each person is using and then explain why. Ask questions such as: *What is this person doing? What senses will they need to do this? Why do they use these senses? Will the person washing their hands just be using the sense of touch?* (No, they will also be smelling the soap, etc.) The students should recognise that some people may be using all of their senses at the same time, whilst others will be using different combinations. Remind the class which sense organ detects which sense, and how that sense can help to protect us.

3 Let the students complete the activity on Workbook page 26. They should draw lines to label the picture and then complete the sentences to describe what each sense does and then draw lines to label the picture. Ask questions as they do this, such as: *What job does the nose do? What job do your eyes do?*

Consolidate and review

● Ask the students to listen to the range of animal sounds on Audio clip B1. Ask: *Could you tell what each one was?* (tiger, gibbons, hawk, donkey, cricket and bird)

● Ask the students to discuss, in their groups, what they have learned about their senses in this unit. After a couple of minutes, take feedback from each group in turn. Write a list of the senses on the board: *sight*, *hearing*, *smell*, *taste*, *touch*. Ask each group to choose one sense and describe it in one sentence.

Differentiation

■ All of the students should be able to correctly match the senses to the sense organs.

● Most of the students should be able to identify the senses that the different people are using. You may need to remind students that it is possible to use more than one sense at a time. Some students may need help in explaining the reasoning. If so, circulate to offer support and guidance as necessary.

▲ Some of the students should be able to label the picture correctly and complete the sentences with little prompting. Others may not be at this level yet, in which case you may need to ask questions to guide them.

2.8 Using our senses

Student's Book pages 40–41

Biology learning objective
- Explore how senses enable humans and animals to be aware of the world around them.

Resources
- Workbook pages 27 and 28
- Slideshow B10: Colours
- Audio clip B2: Familiar sounds
- Audio clip B3: Unfamiliar sounds
- DVD Activity B5: Senses

Classroom equipment
- soft toys
- small plastic containers with small holes in their lids
- cotton-wool balls
- samples of strongly scented substances, such as lemon, orange, vinegar, mint, garlic
- large sheets of paper, coloured pens or pencils

Scientific enquiry skills
- *Ideas and evidence:* Try to answer questions by collecting evidence through observation.

Key words
- **senses**
- **danger**
- **safe**

⚠️ Check if any of the students have food allergies. The students must not eat anything unless they are told that they may. Whenever students are required to taste things in the classroom, hygiene precautions need to be taken. Never give them nuts. If you take the students on a 'sensory hunt' outdoors, ensure they are safe and that they stay together.

Scientific background

Humans and animals have five senses: *touch*, *taste*, *smell*, *sight* and *sound*. These are detected by the sense organs: *skin*, *tongue*, *nose*, *eyes* and *ears*. We use our senses to gather information about our environment and to protect us from danger. Sound travels in waves through the air and into our ears, and causes the eardrum to vibrate. The eye works like a camera. It takes in light from whatever we are looking at and makes a tiny picture of it on the back of the eyeball. When we breathe, air goes into the nose through the nostrils. The tongue is covered with about 10000 taste buds. Each sense organ is connected by nerves to the brain, which tells us the things that our senses detect. The nervous system allows the body to respond to changes in the environment. These responses are usually controlled by the brain and are informed by our senses, which is how they help to keep us safe. At this stage, students do not need to understand the detail of how the body works, but should know that our senses tell us about the world around us and can help keep us from danger.

Introduction

- Ask: *Who can remember all the colours from the previous lesson?* Use the final slide in Slideshow B10 to review the colours. Ask: *What did you eat for your evening meal yesterday? What colours were on your plate? What did the different foods taste like?* Discuss ideas as a class.

- Ask the students to tell you the names of all their senses. If necessary, review the sense organs and the names of the senses, and write them on the board. Ask: *What things do you like to touch? What things do you not like to touch? Why do you like the feel of some things?* Repeat the questions for the other senses.

- Ask the students to look at the picture on Student's Book page 40. Talk about the picture and answer the questions as a class.

Teaching and learning activities

- Ask the students to use their hands to touch something, such as a soft toy. Next, tell them to touch it with their nose, then their cheeks. Ask: *Can you still feel it?* Let them try with their elbows. Say: *You can feel things with your skin all over your body but some places, especially your hands and fingers, can feel things more.* Ask the students: *What else can you tell by using your sense of touch?* Elicit that you can feel hot and cold things, rough and smooth things, hard and soft things.

- Explain that the brain acts very quickly. Say: *If you touch a hot stove it will hurt you, and you will move your hand immediately. This is one way our sense of touch protects us.*

- Put a damp cotton-wool ball into each of the prepared containers. Sprinkle samples of strongly scented substances over the wet cotton-wool balls. (The damp enhances the scent.) Use the same substance in two containers, but make all the rest different. Put the lids on the containers. Ask the students to identify as many scents as they can. They should try to match the two that are the same. Ask: *Were you correct? Was it easy to identify the smells?* Ask the students to suggest words to describe some smells. Take feedback and write the descriptive words on the board for the students to refer to during the lesson. Include *strong*, *weak*, *pleasant*, *unpleasant* as well as more specific terms.

- Direct the students to Student's Book page 41. Let them discuss, in small groups, what they see in the picture. Ask: *What will people see on the street? What sounds will there be? What will the people use to detect danger?* Elicit how our different senses can help to keep us safe.

Graded activities

1 Explain that the students are going to investigate what they can hear. Play Audio clip B2 of eight familiar sounds. Ask the students to identify them. The students should write their answers on Workbook page 27. Then play some unfamiliar sounds from Audio clip B3. Ask the students to describe the sounds, even though they do not know what they are. (fire burning, dolphin calls, keyboard on a computer, a pan of water boiling) Ask: *Is the noise loud or quiet? Is it an animal? Is it a machine? Is it easy to identify sounds when you cannot see what is making them?* Establish that the ear is the organ which detects sounds, and that some sounds are more familiar than others.

2 Divide the class into five groups. Ask each group to choose one of the senses and make a poster to describe that sense and how it helps in our daily lives. Let the groups take turns to present their posters to the class. Ask: *Why do we have senses? What would it be like if we couldn't see, or hear, or feel?* Tell the students that humans who were born without, or who have lost, one of their senses have been found to have developed their other senses more. For example, a blind person's

senses of hearing and smell may be heightened. Ask the students to tell you why they think this happens. Remind the class of how important our senses are for survival.

3 Let the students undertake a 'sensory hunt', inside the classroom or outside. For an indoor activity, add a variety of objects not normally found in the room, for example something that is orange (or another colour), something sweet, something that makes a noise, something with a rough texture and something with an odour. Students should make a list of everything they detect with their senses. Back in the classroom, ask: *Can some objects fit into more than one 'sense' category? Which sense did you use the most? Did you use more than one sense at any time?* Ask students to choose one place they visited and to draw a picture of what their different senses detected there.

Consolidate and review

- Use Workbook page 28 to consolidate the teaching and to check that the students understand that different senses can help us in different situations.

- Let the students complete DVD Activity B5 to consolidate their learning.

Differentiation

■ All of the students should be able to identify a range of familiar and unfamiliar sounds. If some students only know the names in their own language, provide them with the English translations.

● Most of the students should be able to work collaboratively to share ideas and think critically to produce an informative poster about one of the five senses. Most should be able to do this with little help. For those that need some help, you could provide them with a suggested frame on the board, or ask questions to guide their thinking.

▲ Some of the students should be able to list a range of familiar things which their senses detected, such as the sound of other students. More able students may identify less familiar things such as the feel of the surface they are walking on.

2.9 Animal senses

Student's Book pages 42–43

Biology learning objective
- Explore how senses enable humans and animals to be aware of the world around them.

Resources
- Workbook pages 29 and 30
- Slideshow B11: Animal eyes, ears and noses
- Slideshow B12: Animal senses
- Video B9: Hedgehogs

Classroom equipment
- coloured pencils or pens

Scientific enquiry skills
- *Ideas and evidence:* Try to answer questions by collecting evidence through observation.

Key words
- **animal**
- **senses**
- **environment**

Scientific background

Just like humans, animals have senses to detect changes in their environment. These allow them to respond and help to protect them so that they can survive. In the animal kingdom there are many types of eyes and ears, but all eyes give animals vision and all ears give them hearing. Animal skin can be covered in fur or hair (in mammals), feathers (in birds) or scales (in fish and reptiles). The skin protects animals from changes in their environment. Animals' mouths vary in size, shape and dentition, but all mouths allow animals to drink, eat and taste.

In many animals, some senses are more developed than others. Many animals have a very highly developed sense of smell. Their noses can be much more sensitive than human noses. As well as varying in sensitivity, noses also vary in size and shape. Identifying smells is one of the brain's ways of giving us information about our environment. An animal's sense of hearing can also be much stronger than a human's. The human ear is capable of hearing lots of sounds, but not all of them. Some sounds (infrasound) can only be heard by creatures with large ears, such as elephants. Other sounds (ultrasound) can only be detected by animals such as bats, whales, porpoises and dolphins.

At this stage, the students will not learn the specific characteristics or classification of different types of animals, but they do need to understand that senses help tell animals about their environment.

Introduction

- Ask the students to think about their own faces and the faces of some animals that they know. Ask: *What do all humans have that animals have as well?* Let them discuss their answers with a partner. After a short time, check their answers. List them on the board: *ears, eyes, nose, mouth.* (Not all animals have all of these features, but students do not need to know that at this stage.)

- Take the class outside. Tell them to find a space to stand in, and to close their eyes. Explain that you are going to give them some instructions to follow but they must keep their eyes closed tight. Say: *Feel the clothes on your body. Rub the fabrics between your fingers. Think about how they feel. Are they smooth, rough? Do some parts of your body feel cold and some warm? Feel the Sun on your skin. Feel the wind on your skin. Which way does the wind blow? What can you hear? Can you smell any food?* Back in the classroom, ask the students to discuss how important the different senses are. Take feedback as a class.

Teaching and learning activities

- Show the class Slideshow B11, about animals' eyes, ears and noses. Pause after every slide, and discuss the animal and the features shown. Help the students to identify the sense organs and how they can help to protect the animal or help it to find its food. Make sure that they know that the elephant's trunk is its nose. At the end of the slideshow, ask: *What can your nose do?* Let the students talk to each other about it. Repeat the question for eyes and ears. Take feedback and discuss the students' ideas. Encourage them to share their opinions, listen to each other, ask and answer questions.

- Show Video B9 of a hedgehog. Tell the students that many animals have a good sense of smell and that animals' sense of smell is usually much better than ours. Ask: *Which body part do you use to smell things? What smells do you like? What smells do you dislike?* Tell the students that identifying smells is one way we can find out about our environment. Ask: *When could it be useful to have a very good sense of smell?* Explain that animals need a good sense of smell to search for food and help them to find their way around when they have limited vision, such as when it is dark. For big hunters, such as tigers, lions and bears, their food might be quite a distance away. A keen sense of smell allows animals to find food, as well as to stay out of danger. Explain that dogs have such an excellent sense of smell that they can find people quickly and so are often used in search and rescue.

- Ask the students to look at the pictures on Student's Book page 42. Ask them to name the animals shown in the pictures. Ask: *Are the animals' noses alike? In what ways are they different?* Give them time to think about their answers, in groups, before asking for their ideas. Discuss as a class how sight and hearing help animals. Explain that being able to see helps animals to locate food and to move around and avoid hunters. This is true whether they live at the bottom of the ocean, like a dolphin, or soaring high in the sky, like a bird of prey. For more able students you could ask: *Why do animals have two ears?* Ask the students for their ideas and establish that having two ears helps them to hear better.

- Make sure the students understand the questions on Student's Book page 43 and that they recognise the animals in the pictures (snake, butterflies, bat). Work through the questions as a class. Write their ideas on the board. Ensure that they include the suggested answers: a butterfly tastes and touches things with its antennae and feet; a good sense of taste allows animals to find the food they like and protects them from poisonous or rotten food.

Graded activities

1 Let the students complete the activity on Workbook page 29. They should draw lines to match each eye to the animal it belongs to. Circulate to check they are matching correctly, asking questions to guide their thinking.

2 Show the class Slideshow B12 of some different animals in their natural environments. Tell the class about the key sense for each animal and ask how this sense helps the animal to live and grow. Ask them to talk about this in groups. Then discuss each one as a class and elicit the answers: a leopard has a very good sense of smell, so it can find its food; a bat has a very good sense of hearing so it can find its way around at night; a sea urchin has a very good sense of touch to protect itself from big fish; a falcon has a very good sense of sight to see well in the dark and to catch food; a horse has a very good sense of taste to protect itself from eating poisonous plants.

3 Ask the students to choose an animal they have learned about in this lesson. They should draw a picture of it on Workbook page 30. Tell the students to then explain how their chosen animal uses its different senses to survive. Offer support by asking questions: *In what way does it use its sense of smell? Which sense helps it to find food? Do its senses of sight and hearing help it to find food and stay safe?*

Consolidate and review

- Let the students work in their groups to discuss what they have learned about animals' senses. Encourage them to form a sentence about each feature. Take feedback and elicit that all animals have eyes, ears, nose, mouths and skin but that these are very different.

Differentiation

■ All of the students should be able to correctly match each eye to the animal that it belongs to. If necessary, remind students that human beings are animals.

● Most of the students should be able to work together to share ideas, listen to discussions and ask simple questions to describe how senses help the different animals.

▲ Some of the students should be able to draw a reasonable picture of their chosen animal and then give an explanation of how it uses its senses. Circulate, offering support as necessary.

2.10 Babies and adults

Student's Book pages 44–45

Biology learning objective

- Know that humans and animals produce offspring which grow into adults.

Resources

- Workbook page 31
- Slideshow B13: Animals with their young
- (optional) Slideshow B14: Butterfly and frog life cycle
- Slideshow B15: Animals growing up
- DVD Activity B6: How animals change

Classroom equipment

- large sheets of paper
- research materials on animals' life cycles
- coloured pens or pencils

Scientific enquiry skills

- *Ideas and evidence:* Try to answer questions by collecting evidence through observation.
- *Plan investigative work:* Ask questions and contribute to discussions about how to seek answers.
- *Consider evidence and approach:* Make comparisons

Key words

- **have young**
- **adult**
- **baby**
- **offspring**
- **parents**
- **life cycle**

 If the students use the internet, ensure they do so safely and always under adult supervision.

Scientific background

All animals, including humans, reproduce and *have young*. We refer to the *baby* animals produced by the *parents* as *offspring*. All young animals change in some ways as they grow, even if it is just in size. Most animals with which the students are familiar, such as mammals, do not go through significant change as they grow from birth to *adult*. The offspring look very similar to the parents, with similar features, just smaller in size. The young of other animals, such as frogs and butterflies, look very different from the adult animals. These types of animals have different types of bodies at different stages of their *life cycles*. The adult animal is the most well-known stage. In this unit, the students will look at the life cycle of a frog and a butterfly, as well as that of a bird. They will also think about how their own bodies have grown and changed.

Please note that the students do not need to learn about the life cycles of frogs and butterflies for the Cambridge progression tests, this material is additional to the objectives stated by the Cambridge primary framework.

Introduction

- Remind students about what they have learned about plants growing from seeds. Ask: *Do all living things have young? What would happen if an animal*

or plant did not have young? Then take feedback and establish that all living things have young.

- Ask the students to look at the picture on Student's Book page 44. Ask them to find the young animals in the picture and then discuss as a class how they knew which ones were the young animals. Ask: *Do you know which animal each baby animal belongs to? Why do you think this?* Discuss the students' ideas as a class and establish that, in this case, the young animals all look similar to their parents.

- Introduce the key words to the class. Explain to the students that they are now going to learn about offspring and how young animals change as they grow.

Teaching and learning activities

- Ask the students how they have changed since they were born. Ask: *In what ways have you changed as you have got older? Are your arms and legs different from when you were a baby?* Take feedback from the groups. Explain that all animals go through a life cycle and that they are just at the beginning of theirs.

- Having established that humans change as they get older, remind the students that all animals have young. Ask the students to think about how animals change. Show the class Slideshow B13, of some animals and their young.

- Ask the students to look at the picture of frogs and tadpoles on Student's Book page 44. Ask: *Who has seen a tadpole?* Students may have seen tadpoles in ponds, in tanks, on television or in a book. Ask the students what the tadpole eventually becomes. Most will be able to tell you that they change into frogs. Explain that some young animals, such as frogs, look very different from their parents.

- (Please note that the following is an optional activity. The students do not need to learn about the life cycles of frogs and butterflies for the Cambridge progression tests, the material is only included here to support the objectives stated by the Cambridge Primary framework for science.) Show the class the first part of Slideshow B14, the life cycle of the butterfly. Encourage the students to ask questions about what they see. Show the second part of the slideshow, which covers the life cycle of the frog. Discuss and encourage the students to ask questions. Explain that some animals, such as insects, go through a big change when they grow from a baby to an adult, and that the young can look very different from their parents.

- Ask the students to look at the pictures on Student's Book page 45. Let them describe to a partner what is happening at each stage of the bird's life cycle. Ask: *What can the baby bird do for itself? What does it need its parents to help it do?* Explain that some young animals, including human babies, cannot look after themselves until they are older. Ask: *What makes human babies different from the young of animals?* Ask the students to make a list of things that human babies need help with.

Graded activities

1 Let the students complete the activity on Workbook page 31. They should draw lines to match each baby animal to the family it belongs with. This activity encourages the students to think about what some other animals look like when they are young. Circulate to check they are matching correctly, asking questions to guide their thinking.

2 Show the class Slideshow B15, of young animals changing as they grow. Ask the students to identify the animals. Ask: *Do the animals change as they get older?* The students should say that they do. Tell the students to each choose one animal from the slideshow and to draw both the parent and the baby. They should then explain to a partner how that animal changes as it grows.

Then ask the class: *Can you describe how these animals change as they become adults? Do all young animals change this much?* Take feedback and discuss as a class.

3 Tell the students they are going to work in groups to make a poster about the life cycle of an animal. Ask them to choose an animal. They can use an animal they have seen in the lesson or another animal of their choice. Give the students some books, CD-ROMs or allow them to use the internet to research the animal's life cycle. Give each group a large sheet of paper and some coloured pens. They should make a large, illustrated poster to show what they have found out. They should include pictures to show how the animal changes and write a sentence to describe each change. Show them how to use arrows to show the progression from one stage to the next.

Consolidate and review

- Give each group a piece of paper with three circles on it, labelled 'Animals need to eat', 'Animals have senses' and 'Young animals grow into adults'. Ask the students to work together to write, in the correct circles, what they have learned in this topic.

- Let the students complete DVD Activity B6 to consolidate their learning.

Differentiation

■ All of the students should be able to correctly match each baby animal to its family.

● Most of the students should be able to draw a reasonable picture of their chosen animal and describe a range of difference between the young and adult animal. They should be able to name the obvious changes, such as the animal getting bigger, etc. More able students may give less obvious physical changes or discuss changes in ability, such as the animal being able to find its own food.

▲ Some of the students should be able to work collaboratively to carry out their research, asking and answering questions to establish the life cycle of their chosen animal. The drawings themselves are not as important as the understanding of the different stages of growth that the animal goes though. Some students may not be working at this level yet. If so, you may prefer to do this as a more structured activity.

45

Consolidation

Student's Book page 46
Biology learning objectives
- Recognise the similarities and differences between each other.
- Recognise and name the main external parts of the body.
- Know about the need for a healthy diet, including the right types of food and water.
- Explore how senses enable humans and animals to be aware of the world around them.
- Know that humans and animals produce offspring which grow into adults.

Resources
- Workbook page 32
- Assessment Sheets B4, B5 and B6

Looking back

- Use the summary points on Student's Book page 46 to review the key things that the students have learned in the topic. Ask questions such as: *In what ways are you similar to your classmates? In what ways are you different? Can you name the different parts of your body? What are your favourite healthy foods? What is a balanced diet? Where can we find clean water to drink? What do your eyes, ears, nose, tongue and skin help you to do? Describe how you are different now from when you were a baby.*

- Ask the students to look at the picture on Workbook page 32. Discuss it as a class. Ask: *Have you ever been to a fun fair or festival?* Tell them to imagine they are at the fair. Ask: *What would you see? What would you hear? What would you feel? What would you smell? What would you taste?* Allow them time to discuss this in groups. Then ask the students to write what the children in the picture can see, hear and smell at the fun-fair. This activity will show you how well the students have understood the topic.

How well do you remember?

You may use the revision and consolidation activities on Student's Book page 46, either as a test or as a paired class activity. If you are using the activities as a test, have the students work on their own to complete the tasks in writing, and then collect and mark the work. If you are using them as a class activity, you may prefer to let the students do the tasks orally. Circulate as they discuss the questions and observe the students carefully to see who is confident and who is unsure of the concepts.

Some suggested answers

1 Ice-cream, candy floss, popcorn, lollipops, hotdogs, crisps; these foods would be considered unhealthy if eaten in large quantities but are fine to eat occasionally.
2 The children can see other people, fairground rides, food stalls, balloons. They can hear music, people talking and laughing, sounds from the rides. They can smell food from the food stalls.
3 Humans have senses to help inform us of our environment and keep us safe; students' own answers.

Assessment

A more formal assessment of the students' understanding of the topic can be undertaken using Assessment Sheets B4, B5 and B6. This can be completed in class or as a homework task.

Students following Cambridge Primary Science Framework will write progression tests set and supplied by Cambridge Assessment International Education at this level and feedback will be given regarding their achievement levels.

Assessment Sheet answers

Sheet B4
1 Students' labelled drawings. [8]
2 Students' own answers. [2]

Sheet B5
1 Students' own answers. [2]
2 Students' own answers. [2]
3 Fruit [1] It is healthy./The others are unhealthy. [1]
4 source, salt [2]
5 True, false [2]

Sheet B6
1 sight – eyes, touch – hands, smell – nose, hearing – ears [4]
2 George and Charlie [1], George [1], Charlie and Sam [1]
3 look, listen, safe [3]

Student's Book answers

Pages 26–27

1 Children, parents, grandparents, men, women, baby, girl, boy.
2 They all have two eyes, two ears, a nose, a mouth, a body, etc.
3 They both have a mouth, a nose, a body, two eyes, two ears, etc.

Pages 28–29

1 They all have a mouth, a nose, a body, two eyes, two ears, etc.
2 They are different heights, they have different colour hair, skin, eyes. Two are boys, two are girls.
3 They grow longer and stronger.
4 Answers might include: walk, run, feed myself, dress myself, talk, read, etc.
5 Rebecca.

Pages 30–31

1 Students' own answers.
2 Students' own answers.
3 Answers might include: ears, eyes, noses, mouths, arms, legs, hands, fingers, etc.
4 They are moving, stretching, catching a ball, holding a rope, etc.

Pages 32–33

1 Answers might include: fish, vegetables, fruit, cheese, bread, pulses (dried beans).
2 Answers might include: bread, onions, potatoes, chilli, ginger, pomegranates
3 Students' own answers.

Pages 34–35

1 Yes.
2 Answers might include: fruit, vegetables, rice.
3 The mum is eating the healthiest meal because it has lots of vegetables.
4 She is just eating fries. It is not a balanced meal.
5 They may become unhealthy and overweight.

Pages 36–37

1 Answers might include: bottled water, safe tap water.
2 It is too salty.
3 Students' own answers.
4 Answers might include: turn off taps when cleaning teeth, take a shower instead of a bath, do not use hosepipes, etc.

Pages 38–39

1 She is looking at and smelling the flowers. She is using her eyes and nose.
2 They are eating. They are using their sense of taste.
3 They are using their senses of touch, taste, sight and hearing.
4 Your sense of sight when you look at it. Your sense of touch when you peel it. Your senses of smell and taste when you eat it.
5 You cannot taste things as easily.

Pages 40–41

1 They are using their senses of touch, taste, sight and hearing.
2 They can see the beach, they can hear each other and the seagulls, they can taste the ice creams, they can feel the sand, sun and air around them.
3 Hear: traffic, talking, footsteps, etc. See: people, cars, buildings, etc.
4 Your sense of sight lets you see the traffic. Your sense of hearing lets you listen for traffic or danger.
5 Yes.

Pages 42–43

1 The monkey has a small nose, the elephant has long nose (trunk).
2 So they can see small animals (prey) from far away.
3 To keep them safe from danger; to locate small animals (prey) when they are looking for food.
4 Answers might include: Butterflies taste and touch things with their antennae and feet.
5 Answers might include: So they can taste to see if the food is safe to eat.

Pages 44–45

1 Answers might include: baby goats, chicks, calf, foal, etc.
2 They are smaller than their parents. They look different from their parents (chicks).
3 Answers might include: frog, butterfly.
4 Students' own answers.
5 Answers might include: It gets bigger, its feathers change, its beak grows.
6 Answers might include: They cannot feed or clothe themselves. They cannot move (walk) by themselves.

3.1 Exploring materials

Student's Book pages 48–49

Chemistry learning objective
- Use senses to explore and talk about different materials.

Resources
- Workbook page 33
- Slideshow C1: Materials

Classroom equipment
- selection of objects made from wood, metal, plastic and fabric
- hand lenses (optional)
- blindfolds, large boxes
- wooden craft sticks and glue

Scientific enquiry skills
- *Ideas and evidence:* Try to answer questions by collecting evidence through observation.

Key words
- **material**
- **senses**

⚠ Make sure the students are aware they should not put any of the materials into their mouths. Supervise them carefully when they are handling breakable materials such as glass. They should not handle any objects with sharp edges or points. Supervise the students when they use the craft sticks and glue.

Scientific background

Materials are the matter from which things are made. Materials may come from animals (for example, fur, wool, silk), from plants (for example, cotton, straw, linen, wood) or from minerals (for example, stone, metal, rock). Some materials are made from other materials (for example, paper, concrete, iron). Many materials are mixtures of different substances.

Materials can be classified as naturally occurring or not naturally occurring. Materials that are not naturally occurring are manufactured or artificial. For example, crude oil is a naturally occurring raw material from which manufactured materials, such as plastics, dyes and medicines, are derived.

Humans have five senses: *touch*, *taste*, *smell*, *sight* and *sound*. These are detected by the sense organs: *skin*, *tongue*, *nose*, *eyes* and *ears*. We use our senses to gather information about our environment, so we can use them to explore materials in order to find out more about them. Students will learn the names of some common materials and their different properties (characteristics) later in the topic. In this first unit, they will simply use their senses to explore a range of different materials. Students will not be introduced to the concepts of naturally occurring and manufactured (human-made) materials until Stage 2.

Introduction

- Use the topic opener photograph on Student's Book page 47 as a talking point. Ask the students: *What do you think this topic will be about?* Tell them that they are going to learn about different materials and their properties (characteristics).

- Recap what students learned about their senses in Topic 2. Review that our eyes let us see, our ears let us hear, our nose lets us smell, our tongue lets us taste, and our skin lets us feel things. Elicit the names of the five senses and write them on the board.

- Introduce the key words: *material*, *senses*. Write them on the board and point out how each word is spelled and pronounced. Tell the class that they are now going to use their senses to explore some different materials.

Teaching and learning activities

- Show the class Slideshow C1, of different materials. Explain that materials are what objects are made from and that there any many different types of materials in the world. Take one of the materials from the slideshow, for example the piece of wood. Ask questions about its features: *What colour is it? What size is it? What does it look like?* Focus on things the students can easily identify using their sight. Ask: *Which sense are you using?* Stress that we can use our senses to explore materials.

- Show the students a range of objects made from different materials. Allow them a few minutes to explore them by looking, feeling and smelling them. Then ask the students some questions: *Do you know what the object is? What does it feel like? What does it smell like? What do you think it is made from?* Students will learn the names of some common materials in the next unit, so this is not important for this activity. The focus is on students using their senses to describe what they see, feel and smell.

- Encourage them to use as many descriptive words as they can, either in their own language or in English, and compile a class list on the board.

- Establish that we can use different words to describe different materials. Finish by asking: *Which sense did you use for each feature in the list? Which sense did you use the most?*

- Make sure the students understand the questions on Student's Book pages 48–49. Ask them to discuss their answers in groups, then take feedback as a class. For the 'sounds like' question, tell students they should imagine tapping the object with a pencil or on the side of a table. In the 'smells like' question, if the students are unfamiliar with jelly cubes, explain that we mix them with hot water to make a dessert, so they usually smell sweet and fruity.

Graded activities

1 Show the students a range of objects made from different materials. Allow them time to thoroughly explore the objects with their senses. They should handle the materials to feel them (are they heavy or light, rough or smooth?), they should check to see if they have a particular smell, they should look at them from all angles (what shape, size and colour are they?), and tap them gently on the table to see what sound they make. You could provide magnifying hand lenses to allow students to examine them more closely. When they have finished, hold each object up in turn. Ask the students to describe the object, taking ideas from the class until all appropriate descriptive words have been used. Then ask the students to say which sense(s) they used to explore that object.

2 Tell the class they are going to play a game in which they need to try to identify some objects while wearing a blindfold. Before you start, ask the students whether they think it will be harder to identify the objects when they cannot see them. Ask: *Which senses will you use if you cannot use your sense of sight?* Ask the students to work in groups. Students should take turns to wear a blindfold and stand in front of a box of mixed items made from different materials. Ask them to take one item from the box and describe it. Remind them to use their senses of touch, smell and hearing to help them identify the object. (Students should be told not to use their sense of taste.) Ask them to say what they think the object is.

3 Provide the students with a range of objects made from different materials. Allow them time to explore the objects. Then ask them to choose three objects from the selection. Tell them that they need to draw each one on Workbook page 33 and use their senses to help them describe how it looks, feels and sounds. Encourage the students to use as many descriptive words as possible. Point out that they can use the class list on the board for ideas.

Consolidate and review

- Let the students play with some different materials in groups and use them to make up a story.

- Provide some wooden craft sticks and some glue. Ask the students to work with a partner. What can they make out of the wooden pieces?

Differentiation

■ All of the students should be able to use some everyday adjectives to describe the objects, such as those relating to size, shape and colour, and then say which sense they used. More able students may begin to use the property words they will meet in the next unit, such as *hard*, *soft*, *rough*, *smooth*.

● Most of the students should be able to predict the outcome of the game: that it will be harder to identify objects when you cannot see them. Most of the students should be able to use a range of familiar and less familiar descriptive words for the objects and have a good guess at what the object is by using their sense of touch. More able students may also use their senses of smell and hearing to help them.

▲ Some of the students should be able to accurately describe their chosen objects. For those who need some prompting, circulate, asking questions to guide their thinking.

3.2 Properties of materials

Student's Book pages 50–51

Chemistry learning objective
- Identify the characteristics of different materials.

Resources
- Workbook pages 34 and 35
- PCM C1: Describing materials
- DVD Activity C1: Colours and textures

Classroom equipment
- wooden blocks
- selection of objects of different sizes and weights, simple means of weighing them
- paper bag, strong plastic bag
- metal paperclips, metal spoons
- large sheets of paper, coloured pens or pencils
- wide strips of cotton, wool, fleece, plastic, wood (ruler), steel (bar), rope (natural) and elastic
- loads with equal mass (e.g. marbles), plastic containers, small pieces of string, eye protection, large box
- range of materials for collages, glue

Scientific enquiry skills
- *Ideas and evidence:* Try to answer questions by collecting evidence through observation.

- *Plan investigative work:* Ask questions and contribute to discussions about how to seek answers; make predictions.
- *Obtain and present evidence:* Explore and observe in order to collect evidence (measurements and observations) to answer questions; suggest ideas and follow instructions; record stages in work.
- *Consider evidence and approach:* Make comparisons; compare what happened with predictions.

Key word
- **properties**

⚠ Supervise students when they are handling breakable materials such as glass. They should not handle any objects with sharp edges or points. Make sure that the students use the strength test apparatus correctly and safely. Provide the students with eye protection and put a large box on the floor to catch the weights. Make sure that the students use lengths of materials that end about 10 cm above the floor. Advise the students to take care not to drop the load onto fingers or the floor.

Scientific background

Materials are classified according to their *properties*. There are many different properties: some are visible, some are determined by investigation or by using special equipment. The main visible properties are colour, transparency and texture. Less obvious properties include hardness, strength, flexibility and elasticity. The properties of a material determine its suitability for a particular purpose. Often several properties are taken into consideration, including cost and availability.

Introduction

- Ask the class to look at the pictures on Student's Book page 50. Ask: *What do the different materials look like? What words would you use to describe them? In what ways are they different?* Encourage the students to use a range of suitable adjectives

to describe them. The purpose of this activity is to assess the students' existing knowledge.

- Introduce and discuss the key word *property*. Show the class a material, for example a piece of wood. Ask: *What colour is it? What size is it? What does it look like?* Explain that colour is a property of a material. Write the word on the board.

- Introduce more key words: *hard, soft, heavy, light, strong, weak, shiny, dull, rough, smooth*. Write them on the board and explain what each word means. Say we use these words to describe more properties of materials: the way they look and the way they feel.

Teaching and learning activities

- Point out some examples of *hard* materials around the classroom (e.g. wood, metal, plastic, glass). Give the students time to look at them. Then ask about *soft* materials (e.g. cotton, rubber, paper) and ask individuals for their ideas. Show the students two very different materials, for example a cotton t-shirt and a glass, and ask: *Which is harder?* Discuss the questions on Student's Book page 50 as a class. Establish why some objects need to be hard.

- Ask: *What do we mean if we say something is heavy or light?* Show the class a range of different objects. Ask a volunteer to put the objects in order, heavy to light, just by looking at them. Encourage the other students to comment. Ask: *Is there any pattern to the order?* It is likely that most of the big objects are placed as the heaviest and the small objects as the lightest. Check by weighing and move the objects so they are in the correct order of weight. Ask: *What is surprising about the order now?* Establish that heavy things do not always need to be big.

- Direct the students to Student's Book page 51 and discuss the picture. Ask: *What has happened?* (The bag was not strong enough to carry the shopping, it has broken.) Give the students two bags, one made of paper and one made of fairly strong plastic. Ask: *Which bag is stronger? Explain why we know which is stronger?*

- Give each pair of students a set of cards cut from PCM C1 of different property words. Show the students a range of objects made from different materials. Ask them to describe the objects, using words on the cards, such as *hard, soft, shiny, dull*. Select different students to place a property word card with an object it belongs to. Some can be used more than once. Encourage them to give reasons for their choices. (Note that at this stage, the students do not need to be able to name the material that each object is made from, just to match the property words we use to describe them.)

- Make sure the students understand the question on Student's Book page 51. Ask them to discuss their answers in groups, then take feedback.

Graded activities

1 Give each pair of students some coloured pens and a large sheet of paper. Ask them to divide the paper into four equal sections. Tell them that they should make a poster to show four different objects: a hard object, a soft object, a smooth object and a rough object. They should choose an object that matches each property and draw a picture of it in that section of the poster. They can select from the objects they have seen in this lesson or any suitable alternative. Encourage them to add labels with each property name and the name of the object.

2 Ask the students to work in small groups. Give each group a metal paperclip and a metal spoon. Direct the students to Workbook page 34 and explain the activity. When they have completed the table, ask: *What have you found out?* Establish the properties the metals have in common and their differences.

3 Show the class the strips of different materials and ask: *Which do you think will be the strongest?* Take a class vote and put their predictions on the board. Set up the apparatus, as shown on Workbook page 35. Show the students what to do, starting with one weight in the container and adding further weights one at a time. Say that they will be testing the strips of different materials. Show them how to connect the load properly. Remind them that the test must be fair, so the strips must be the same size and that the investigation ends when the material being tested is broken, not when the load falls off. Give the students time to do the investigation. They should record their results on Workbook page 35. Ask the students to use their results to rank the materials in order, strongest to weakest. Ask: *Which was the strongest/weakest material? Were they all the same? Why? Was the test fair?* Ask them if their results showed their prediction to be correct. Ask them to give reasons for their answer.

Consolidate and review

- Give the students a selection of materials with different textures to make a collage with. They should select materials appropriately, such as for example using sandpaper (rough) for a beach, aluminium foil (shiny) for a spaceship.

- Let the students complete DVD Activity C1 to consolidate their learning.

Differentiation

■ All of the students should be able to identify an object for each of the four properties with little prompting.

● Most of the students should be able to work together, asking and answering questions and using first-hand observations to compare the two objects.

▲ Some of the students should be able to make predictions about the outcome of an investigation and then follow instructions to find out if they were correct.

3.3 More properties

Student's Book pages 52–53

Chemistry learning objective
• Identify the characteristics of different materials.

Resources
• Workbook pages 36, 37 and 38
• PCM C2: Cardboard glasses

Classroom equipment
• glass object
• cup of water, selection of absorbent and less absorbent materials, such as sponges, dish cloths, paper towels, tissues, nylon, cotton, wool, polyester
• yoghurt pots with a hole in the base, teaspoons or syringes for measuring out small fixed amounts of water, paper towels, sand timers
• samples of a selection of materials, such as cotton, wool, sugar paper, newspaper, aluminium foil, plastic (yoghurt pots with a hole in the base, samples of materials large enough to cover the hole in the yoghurt pot and go part way up the side)
• selection of different transparent plastics, sticky tape

Scientific enquiry skills
• *Ideas and evidence:* Try to answer questions by collecting evidence through observation.
• *Plan investigative work:* Make predictions.
• *Obtain and present evidence:* Explore and observe in order to collect evidence (measurements and observations) to answer questions; suggest ideas and follow instructions; record stages in work.
• *Consider evidence and approach:* Make comparisons; compare what happened with predictions.

Key words
• **see-through** • **stretch** • **flexible**
• **absorbent** • **elastic**
• **waterproof** • **bend**

⚠ Supervise students when they are handling breakable materials such as glass. They should not handle any objects with sharp edges or points.

Scientific background

The property of transparency (see-through) refers to letting light through. This means that the light rays pass through the material without being changed in any way. Glass, some plastics, air and water have this property. *Transparent* materials can be coloured. Some materials are *waterproof*, meaning they do not allow water to penetrate or pass through them. Some materials are coated with a substance that makes them waterproof but the material itself is not waterproof. Substances such as rubber, wax and polyurethane are such coating materials. Materials that are not waterproof absorb water; *absorbent* materials soak up water and become wet. Absorbent materials are useful for a range of purposes, such as clearing up spillages and keeping things moist. Some materials are stretchy or *elastic*: they can be *stretched* but will return to the original shape once the force has been removed. The fabric that is called 'elastic' is not the only material that has this property. Many other materials have elastic properties and they are used for many things, from clothes to car tyres. Some materials can be squashed or *bent*. Others

cannot. A material that is very squashy and bendy is *flexible*.

Different properties make materials suitable for certain uses, but unsuitable for others.

Introduction

● Review the key word from the previous lesson, *property*. Show the class an object made of glass. Ask: *What properties does this object have? What words would you use to describe it?* Write the students' suggestions on the board. Ask questions to elicit that we can see through glass. Tell students that the property word for this feature is *see-through*. Tell them that they are now going to learn about some more properties of different materials.

● Introduce some more key words for this unit and explain what each word means. Write them on the board.

Teaching and learning activities

● Ask the students to look at the picture on Student's Book page 52. As a class, discuss the see-through objects in the picture and establish that see-through materials are used for windows in buildings and vehicles. Although the word *glass* is not introduced until the next unit, most students will be familiar with this material from everyday life. Ask the students to think of as many different uses of glass as they can and make a class list on the board. Ask the students to decide what properties of glass give it so many different uses. Elicit that glass is *see-through* so it is very suitable for making things such as windows.

● Ask: *What does waterproof mean?* Explain that some materials (e.g. rubber) are waterproof and do not let water through them. Spill a small cup of water on the floor, in front of the class. Ask the students to suggest how to clear it up. Use some of their ideas and try out a range of different materials. Then ask: *Why was the paper towel (or sponge or tissue) useful for clearing up the water? Was the paper towel waterproof? Why do you think this?* Discuss the word *absorbent* and clarify its meaning, using the demonstration as an example to show that it means to able to take in water. Then ask the students to answer the questions on Student's Book page 52.

● Establish that the term *flexible* refers to a material that can bend easily without breaking. Ask the students to think of as many uses for flexible materials as they can. List them on the board. Ask the students: *Are flexible materials strong or weak? Think of uses for strong and weak flexible materials. Think of uses where flexibility would not be a good thing.* Discuss students' ideas and correct any misconceptions.

● Make sure the students understand the questions on Student's Book page 53. Allow them to discuss their answer in groups, then take feedback.

Graded activities

1 Ask the students to complete the activity on Workbook page 36. They should look at the different objects and decide which property word(s) best describe each one. Circulate to check that they are matching the correct words to each object. Ask questions to guide their thinking. Once they have completed the activity, you can ask them to explain their reasoning.

2 Show the students a selection of absorbent materials, such as sponges, paper towels, hand towels, mops. Tell them to choose three of them. They should then draw and label a picture of each

one on Workbook page 37 and say what each material can be used for. Recap that they are all used for soaking up water, or other liquids. Ask: *What do you think happens to the water? What property word do we use for a material that can do this?*

3 Tell the class they are going to test some materials to find out which is best for making an umbrella. Demonstrate the investigation to test how waterproof the materials are, as shown on Workbook page 38. Put a piece of material over the bottom of a yoghurt pot in which a hole has been made. Stand the yoghurt pot on a paper towel. Add a fixed amount of water (from a teaspoon or syringe) and after a certain time look to see if any water has soaked onto the paper towel. Ask the students to carry out the investigation in their groups. Keep reminding the students of the need for fair testing. Check that each group is working as a team, with the same ideas. Visit each group and ask if they can predict which fabric will be the most waterproof. Using their results, discuss which material would be best for making an umbrella. Ask: *Why do you think this? Does everyone agree?* Discuss the students' reasons. Ask: *What properties does material for an umbrella need to have?* Take feedback, ensuring that *waterproof* is one of the properties listed.

Consolidate and review

● Help the students make some glasses out of see-through plastic. Have some cardboard frames already cut from PCM C2. The students use tape to stick the different plastics onto the frames. Allow them to vote on which are the best.

Differentiation

■ All of the students should be able to correctly match the property words to each object.

● Most of the students should be able to draw a reasonable representation of each material and label it correctly. Most students should be able to identify uses of each material with little prompting.

▲ Some of the students should be able to make predictions about the outcome of the investigation and then follow instructions to find out if they were correct. Offer support and guidance to students who may not be at this level yet.

3.4 What material is it?

Student's Book pages 54–55

Chemistry learning objective
- Recognise and name common materials.

Resources
- Workbook pages 39 and 40
- Slideshow C2: Wood
- Video C1: Glass shaping

Classroom equipment
- samples of different materials: as many as possible from wood, stone, paper, cardboard, fabric, wool, cotton, metal, plastic, glass
- range of objects made from glass, such as beaker, thermometer, drinking glass and bottle
- selection of different objects made from wood
- selection of objects made from wood, metal, fabric and plastic

Scientific enquiry skills
- *Ideas and evidence:* Try to answer questions by collecting evidence through observation.

Key word
- material

⚠️ Supervise students carefully when they are handling breakable materials such as glass. They should not handle any objects with sharp edges or points.

Scientific background

There are many different types of materials. This unit will introduce the students to some of the more common materials such as *wood*, *wool*, *cotton*, *metal*, *plastic* and *glass*. *Wood* comes from trees and is very useful. *Paper* and *cardboard* are made from wood. *Stone* is quarried from rock faces. Stone is very hard and strong so is often used for making things such as building blocks and paving stones. *Fabric* is the generic term used for types of cloth or textile. Fabrics made from fibres originating from plants and animals include *cotton* (from cotton plant) and *wool*. Wool is the generic term for fibres obtained from sheep and certain other animals. There are also manufactured fibres, such as nylon and polyester, which the students will look at in more detail in Unit 3.7. *Metals* are materials that come from rocks called metal ores. Metals are very hard, strong and shiny and can be made into many different things. There are many different types of metals, some with unique properties. *Plastics* are made from crude oil. Plastics are chemically manufactured to have different properties and can be shaped and moulded, making them suitable for a very wide range of uses. *Glass* is an unusual material. It is made from sand, sodium carbonate and limestone, heated to a high temperature and cooled. Most glass is transparent so it is usually used to make windows. At this stage, the students will learn the names of these materials and relate them to properties they learned in previous units; they do not need to understand how the materials are sourced or made.

Introduction

● Introduce the key word *materials*. Then introduce some examples of different materials: *wood*, *stone*, *paper*, *cardboard*, *fabric*, *wool*, *cotton*, *metal*, *plastic*, *glass*. Write them on the board and point out how each word is spelled and pronounced. Explain that there are many different types of materials in the world and that these are the names of a few common materials. Students may already be familiar with some of the names.

● Point to objects in the classroom. Ask the class to identify each object and the material it is made from, for example, a window made from glass. Stress that wood, cotton, metal, etc. are all *materials*. Emphasise the difference between what an object is (and is used for) and the material it is made from. For example, say: *This is a spoon. It is used for eating. It is made from metal.* Have some samples of materials that have not been made into everyday objects, for example, pieces of plastic, wood, metal, to help identify the material and distinguish it from the object.

Teaching and learning activities

● Ask the students to look at the picture on Student's Book page 54. Ask what they can see in the bedroom, what each object is and what they think it is made from. Discuss their ideas as a class. Then allow the students time to answer the questions in their groups.

Take feedback and elicit the objects made from wood and plastic, and the different uses of fabrics.

● Show the students some objects made from wood, for example, a table, chairs, a spoon. Ask the class where wood comes from. Elicit that wood is obtained from trees. Show the class Slideshow C2, of trees being felled and some wooden products. Ask the students to think of some ways in which we use wood every day. Establish that wood can be shaped into many different shapes. Point to a chair and say: *Even though it has been made into an object, it is still wood; it came from a tree.* Explain that wood is also used to make cardboard and paper.

● Show the students some objects made from glass. Include a beaker, a glass thermometer, a drinking glass and a bottle. Explain that a lot of glass is blown into shape, either by mouth or by machine. Show Video C1, of glass shaping and how it can be formed into different shapes. Ask: *What did the man make from glass?* Ask the students to think of as many different uses of glass as they can. Make a class list. Ask the students to look at the different uses and decide what properties of glass give it so many different uses. Establish that glass is *see-through*, which means they can see through it.

● Show the students the range of materials. Call up different students and ask them to take it in turns to select all the plastic objects. Time the students to see who can do this the fastest. Ask if they can think of any uses of plastics at home or in school. They might suggest drinking bottles, glasses, plastic cutlery, plates, mobile phone cases, toys, and so on. Ask: *What makes plastic so useful?*

● Make sure the students understand the questions on Student's Book page 55. Ask them to discuss their answers in groups, then take feedback.

Graded activities

1 Invite the students to go on a materials hunt around the classroom, looking for things made from wood, metal, fabric and plastic. Before the lesson, hide some materials around the classroom for the students to find. The students should look at the pictures on Workbook page 39, and then search for similar items. Ask: *What did you find that is made from this material? Where did you find it? What is the object?*

2 Ask the students to complete the task on Workbook page 40. Ask them to tick the material that would be best for making each object. Remind them to think about the most important property for the object to do its job, and assess which material offers that property.

3 Tell the students that a toy company is making a new car for two-year old children. They want to know which materials they should make it from. Ask the students to discuss this in pairs. Ask: *What materials should they use? Why?* Ask the students to design a toy with their partner, using only wood, metal and plastic. They should say how they would use the materials on these toys. Ask: *Why do you think the materials you have chosen would be the best? Why has this material been used in this way?* You can write a list of suitable property words on the board to help them, such as *hard, soft, strong, rough, smooth, light, flexible, see-through.*

Consolidate and review

● Tell the students you are going to say the names of some objects. Some of them will be made from plastic and some will not. They should stand up when they hear one that can be made from plastic.

● Ask the students to make a fact sheet to show as many different uses of wood (or another material of your choice) as they can.

Differentiation

■ All of the students should be able to locate some objects made from the various different materials and sort them into the correct category.

● Most of the students should be able to think critically to decide which material best suits each object. More able students should be able to explain their reasoning.

▲ Some of the students should be able to work collaboratively to share ideas and think creatively. Students should be able to choose appropriate materials for the different parts of their toy and then provide reasons, demonstrating that they have understood the properties that make the materials best suited for that job.

3.5 **More materials**

Student's Book pages 56–57

Chemistry learning objective

- Recognise and name common materials.

Resources

- Workbook page 41
- Video C2: Making concrete
- PCM C3: Concrete or glass?
- DVD Activity C2: Metal, wood, plastic

Classroom equipment

- cards, large sheets of paper
- selection of objects made from wood, metal, stone, fabric, leather and rubber
- pictures of different bridges, materials for making model bridges, such as drinking straws, cocktail sticks, rope or string, sheets of paper, modelling clay, corrugated card, etc.
- coloured pens, scissors, glue, old magazines
- real objects as on Workbook page 41 if possible
- toy car

Scientific enquiry skills

- *Plan investigative work:* Decide what to do to try to answer a science question.
- *Obtain and present evidence:* Suggest ideas and follow instructions.
- *Consider evidence and approach:* Model and communicate ideas in order to share, explain and develop them.

Key word

- **material**

⚠️ Supervise the students when they use scissors and glue. If you take the students on a walk around the school grounds, ensure they are safe and that they stay together.

Scientific background

Concrete is a human-made (manufactured) material. *Clay* is a type of heavy, sticky soil that becomes hard when it is baked. It is often used to make *brick*. Natural *rubber* is made from a liquid called latex that comes from certain plants. Manufacturing processes are used to turn latex into a much more versatile material. About 30% of the rubber used today is natural rubber. The other 70% comes from crude oil, from which the rubber is made synthetically. *Leather* is a durable and flexible material, created by tanning animal hide or skin, commonly from cattle.

Sometimes materials may be combined to produce a new material that has different properties. For example, copper is a soft metal and zinc is rather brittle, but together they make the alloy brass, which is hard and tough. Manufacturing often involves a change that leads to a new set of desired characteristics. An example of a modern, manufactured material is that used for airbags in the safety systems of many cars. In the event of an accident, these inflate automatically to protect the driver and passengers. Airbags must be made of very flexible material, so they can blow up quickly. They also need to be strong, so they do not burst under impact.

Introduction

- Ask the students to discuss what a material is and to name some different materials from the previous lesson. It is important to ensure that the students have understood that *materials* are not just fabrics or cloths. Make a list on the board of common materials from the previous lesson.

- Remind the students what wood, metal, stone and fabric look like. Show them an object made from each material and ask: *What is this object made from?* Then introduce the words *concrete*, *brick*, *clay*, *rubber*, *leather*, and explain that they are the names of some more common materials. Write the words on the board and point out how each word is spelled and pronounced.

- Ask the students to select one of the materials from the board and write its name on a piece of card. Describe your journey to school and ask them to hold up their card every time an object is mentioned that is made from their material.

Teaching and learning activities

- Show the students objects that are made from rubber and leather, and ask them to describe the differences between the two materials. Ask the students to look at the picture on Student's Book page 56. Ask: *Can you think of any other uses of rubber and leather?*

● Show the class Video C2 about how concrete is made. Explain that once the concrete is made, it can be moulded into different shapes, such as blocks or paving stones, and left to set into shape. Discuss some uses of concrete with the students.

● Tell the students they are going to go on a tour of the school grounds. Let them first make some predictions about the concrete or glass objects they might see. Ask them to record their predictions on PCM C3. They should add to their lists any other objects that they did not predict. Discuss what the students found out on their tour. Ask: *Which of your predictions were correct? Which were not correct? Why was this? Did you find many objects that you did not expect? Which material was more common, concrete or glass? Why do you think this was?*

● Ask the students to look at the pictures on Student's Book pages 56–57. Talk about the modern materials used to make the helmet, the food box and the tablet. Allow the students some time to work in groups to try to identify some of the materials used. Discuss the reasons for using these materials. Ask the students if any other materials could have been used instead and discuss their responses.

Graded activities

1 Give each student a sheet of paper and some coloured pens. Ask: *Where does wood come from? What other materials are made from wood? What would happen if there was no more wood?* Tell them to imagine a future world with no wood or wood products. Ask them to draw a picture of what their bedroom would look like. Circulate to make sure they are not drawing anything that is made from wood. Ask questions such as: *If we cannot use wood to make a bed frame, what could we use instead?*

2 Ask the students to complete the task on Workbook page 41. Ask them to look at the pictures of some objects made from three modern materials. If they are unfamiliar with the materials, explain what each one is. If possible, bring an example of each to class for the students to explore. Students should then circle two property words for each object. Remind them to think about the most important properties for the object to do its job. Once they have done this, ask them to name one different use for each material.

3 Show the class some pictures of different bridges. Ask the students to identify the materials used for each of them. Establish that the main materials for building bridges are metal, concrete and wood. Tell the students that they are going to try making their own bridges out of different materials. The bridge should be about 20 cm long and 10 cm wide. Show them these dimensions. Give each group some materials. Ask them to work together to design a bridge that will stand up and support the weight of a toy car going over it. Ask the students to display their bridges to the class. Ask the class to predict which will be the strongest bridge.

Consolidate and review

● Arrange the students into groups. Give them two large sheets of paper, scissors, glue and some old magazines. Ask them to put the title *Metal* on one sheet of paper and *Concrete* on the other. Ask them to cut out pictures of objects made from metal or concrete and to plan a collage or display of materials. Ask them to describe the objects and say what they are used for.

● Let the students complete DVD Activity C2 to consolidate their learning.

Differentiation

■ All of the students should be able to think creatively and relate this to what they have learned about wood and its various uses. Students should also be able to use their knowledge of properties of other materials to suggest suitable replacements for wooden objects, such as a metal bed frame.

● Most of the students should be able to choose the correct properties that match each modern material. Some may need a little prompting if they are unfamiliar with the objects shown.

▲ Some of the students should be able to work collaboratively to share ideas and think creatively about which materials to use in their bridge design. More-able students will use a wider range of materials and less-able students will use materials they are most familiar with. As long as students give sensible reasoning for their choice of materials, there are no right or wrong answers, and all designs should be encouraged.

3.6 Sorting materials

Student's Book pages 58–59

Chemistry learning objective

- Sort objects into groups based on the properties of their materials.

Resources

- Workbook pages 42–43 and 44
- PCM C1: Describing materials
- PCM C4: Sorting materials

Classroom equipment

- selection of objects made from wood, metal, stone, plastic, glass and fabric
- drinking glass, glass vase
- old magazines, scissors, glue

- wooden bricks or blocks, of different sizes, shapes and colours

Scientific enquiry skills

- *Ideas and evidence:* Try to answer questions by collecting evidence through observation.

Key words

- **sort**
- **group**
- **properties**

⚠ Supervise the students when they use scissors and glue. Supervise them carefully when they are handling breakable materials such as glass. They should not handle any objects with sharp edges or points.

Scientific background

Materials are classified according to their *properties*. There are many different properties: some are visible, some are determined by investigation or by using special equipment. The main visible properties are colour, transparency and texture. Less obvious properties include strength, hardness, flexibility and elasticity. We can group materials by their type, such as metal or wood, or by a property that they have in common, such as being transparent or smooth. It is sometimes possible to *sort* a material into more than one *group*. This is because a material can have more than one property. For example, wool is both soft and flexible.

Introduction

- Show the students a range of objects from previous lessons. Call up different students and ask them to take it in turns to select a plastic object. When all the plastic objects have been chosen, hold one up and ask: *What made you decide this was a plastic object? What properties does it have?* Arrange all the plastic objects in a group together. Explain that we can sort objects into groups.

- Introduce the key words: *sort, group, properties.* Write them on the board and point out how each word is spelled and pronounced. Ask the students to repeat the words after you. Tell the students to look at the group of plastic objects. Ask: *Are all*

these objects made from plastic? (yes) Establish that we can group objects based on their material.

Teaching and learning activities

- Ask students to look again at the group of plastic objects. Add a drinking glass and a glass vase. Ask: *Are all these objects made from plastic?* (no) Then ask: *Are all these objects see-through?* (Ensure they are.) Establish that we can also group according to different properties. Explain that it is possible for different materials to be grouped together if they share the same property.

- Ask the class to look at the picture on Student's Book page 58. Ask: *What can you see in the picture?* Talk about the different materials and objects in the picture, and answer the questions as a class.

- Using the range of objects from the introduction, call up different students and ask them to take it in turns to pick out all the wooden objects. When all the wooden objects have been chosen, group them together on the table. Then ask the students to pick out all the metal objects, and do the same again. Use this activity to reinforce the concept that objects can be sorted in groups by type of material.

- Give each group a tray with a selection of objects made from different materials, including wood, metal, plastic, fabric, glass and stone. Let them examine the objects and use descriptive words to explain the properties. Take feedback and compile a class list on the board.

● Ask the students to group the materials according to some common properties, for example, hard, soft, shiny, smooth, grey, etc. In each case, ask them to justify their groupings and which objects they have chosen. Ask: *Why have you grouped those together? Is everything in the group made from the same material?* Ask the students to find other ways of grouping the same objects, by using different properties. Use this activity to reinforce the concept that materials can be sorted into groups by property.

● When the students have grouped their materials, ask them to look closely at one of their groups by asking: *Are all the samples of wood the same? Are all the pieces of plastic of the same colour?* It is important that the students begin to see that there are different types of wood, plastic, etc. (They will learn more about this in the next unit.) Emphasise the difference between the object itself and the material it is made from.

● Give each group a set of word cards cut from PCM C1, of different properties. Place wooden, metal, cotton and plastic objects in front of the students. Ask them to place correct property word cards with each material. Some can be used more than once. Encourage them to talk about their choices and to give some examples.

● Make sure the students understand the questions on Student's Book page 59. Let them discuss their answers in groups, then take feedback as a class.

Graded activities

1 Give each group of students a selection of old magazines, some scissors and glue. Ask them to look for some pictures of objects made from wood, metal, plastic and fabric. They should then cut out the pictures and sort them into groups before sticking them in the correct places on Workbook pages 42–43. Remind students that *fabric* covers a wide range of materials, including wool and cotton.

2 Provide the students with a selection of different objects to sort. They should work together to place all of the plastic, metal, stone and fabric objects into separate piles of the same materials. Ask: *What features of the materials made you sort them into these groups?* Talk about the differences

in the materials that help to sort the objects. Ask: *What about the colour of the material? What did the material feel like? Was it a strong material?* Recap the different properties that these materials have. Ask if the students can find more than one way to sort the objects. If necessary, remind them that we can sort by type of material and by property.

3 Ask the students to complete the activity on Workbook page 44. Explain that they need to decide which item is the odd one out, from three given objects or materials. This task is made harder because they also have to give a reason for their ideas. Ask questions to guide their thinking: *What do two of the objects have in common? What are they made from? Where does the material come from? Is it made from metal? What are the objects used for? What do they look like?* This activity helps to develop thinking and reasoning skills.

Consolidate and review

● Give groups of students a selection of wooden bricks. Ask them to sort them into groups of the same size, then the same shape and then the same colour.

● Give pairs of students a copy of cards cut from PCM C4. Ask them to sort the pictures into fabric, metal, wood and stone.

Differentiation

■ All of the students should be able to identify pictures of objects made from the four different materials, and correctly sort them into groups, with little prompting.

● Most of the students should be able to explore the selection of objects and use their acquired knowledge of materials and their properties to sort them into appropriate groups.

▲ Some of the students should be able to think critically to choose which is the odd one out and provide sound reasoning for their choice. Some students may struggle to do this, especially as there is a mix of materials and objects, so circulate and offer support as necessary.

3.7 Making smaller groups

Student's Book pages 60–61

Chemistry learning objective
- Sort objects into groups based on the properties of their materials.

Resources
- Workbook page 45–46 and 47
- Slideshow C3: Traditional clothing
- DVD Activity C3: Human-made materials

Classroom equipment
- different samples of wool, cotton, silk, polyester and nylon
- woollen scarf
- selection of plastic objects, for example plastic bags, plastic bottles, soft plastic film, hard plastic buckets
- selection of different types of paper, for example newspaper, writing paper, poster paper, wrapping paper, cardboard, tissue paper, greaseproof paper and kitchen paper
- small samples of plastic cut from food wrap, plastic bags and plastic bottles
- different types of paper for collages
- scissors, glue

Scientific enquiry skills
- *Ideas and evidence:* Try to answer questions by collecting evidence through observation.
- *Plan investigative work:* Make predictions; decide what to do and try to answer a science question.
- *Obtain and present evidence:* Explore and observe in order to collect evidence (measurements and observations) to answer questions; record stages in work.
- *Consider evidence and approach:* Make comparisons; compare what happened with predictions.

Key word
- **fabric**
- **plastic**

 Supervise the students when they use scissors and glue.

Scientific background

There are different types of some materials. Each type has different properties, so we can sort the different types into smaller groups. For example, *wool*, *cotton*, *silk*, *polyester* and *nylon* are all types of fabric. Different processes are used to make fabrics with different properties, giving them a wide variety of uses.

Plastics are very useful materials because so many different types of plastics can be made, all with particular properties. Some are waterproof, some are heat resistant and some can withstand corrosion from different chemicals, such as acids. Most are light, long-lasting and hardwearing, making them suitable alternatives to metal.

There is a huge variety of different uses for paper, owing to the different properties available. Different chemicals are added to provide different textures and qualities. Examples of paper include cardboard, writing paper, paper bags, tissues, coffee filters, and so on.

At this stage, the students do not need to understand how different types of different materials are made.

They do need to appreciate that the different types exist and that they have different properties, making them suitable for a range of uses.

Introduction

- Introduce some more key words: *wool*, *cotton*, *polyester*, *silk*, *nylon*. Write them on the board and point out how each word is spelled and pronounced. Ask the students to repeat the words after you. Explain that there are different types of some materials and these are all types of *fabric*. Then ask the students to look at the pictures on Student's Book page 60. Ask: *Can you recognise any of the fabrics in the pictures?* Answer the questions as a class.

- Show the students different samples of wool, cotton, silk, polyester and nylon. Ask the students to feel them and to compare the similarities and differences between the materials. Encourage them to use property words that they learned earlier in the topic, such as *soft*, *flexible*, *smooth*, etc. Tell the class that they are now going to learn about different types of fabric, plastic and paper.

Teaching and learning activities

● Ask the students: *Where does wool come from?* Show them a scarf or something else made from wool. Discuss with the students the fact that, even though it has been made into an object, it is still wool. Explain that wool often comes from sheep.

● Ask the students to look at the pictures at the bottom of Student's Book page 60. Ask: *What do you know about plastics?* Take answers and discuss some of the properties of plastics (flexible, soft, hard, see-through, etc.) Ask: *Why are plastics so useful? Name some of the many different ways we use plastics.* Make sure the students understand that there are many different types of plastics, each with different properties and uses. Illustrate this with a selection of different plastic objects. Explain that these objects are all made from plastic, but the plastic has been chosen to have different properties. Allow the students time to explore the objects. Ask: *In what ways are they similar? In what ways are they different? What do we use each one for?* Ask them to sort the different types of plastics into groups based on their own choice of criteria.

● Show the class a range of different types of paper. Invite the students to feel the paper samples and describe their properties. Ask: *Where does paper come from?* (trees) *Why do we need so many different sorts of paper?* (It has many different properties and therefore uses.)

● Direct the students to Student's Book page 61. Ask: *What is the girl in the picture doing? What type of paper do you think she is using?*

Graded activities

1 Show the students Slideshow C3, of different traditional clothing and costumes from around the world. Encourage them to ask questions about the images. Prompt them to describe the colours and textures of the different clothes the people are wearing. Ask: *Can you think of any other uses of fabrics?* Write a class list on the board.

2 Tell the class they are going to investigate different types of paper. Provide them with a selection of papers to explore. Then tell them they should write the properties of each one on Workbook page 45 and try to name the specific types of paper. Some may only be able to do this in their own language,

so provide English translations as necessary. Then ask them to choose six different types of paper and to glue them on Workbook page 46. Finally, the students should say which paper they think is the strongest, thinnest, smoothest, heaviest, shiniest and most flexible.

3 Tell the class they are going to investigate different types of plastic. Provide the students with samples of food wrap, plastic bags and plastic from plastic bottles ready cut into pieces. Ask the students to work together to test each piece of plastic by a) trying to look through it, b) stretching it, c) trying to break it. They should record their results on Workbook page 47. Take feedback as a class and discuss their findings.

Consolidate and review

● Ask the students to work in small groups to make a poster about an environment of their choice using different types of paper. Let them first talk about their ideas. Ask: *What types of paper will you use and why?* If they are struggling, you could suggest they use shiny paper for metals, blue tissue paper for water, corrugated cardboard for wood. Let the students come up with more ideas of their own. Once they have agreed on a plan, ask them to make their poster.

● Let the students complete DVD Activity C3 to consolidate their learning.

Differentiation

■ All of the students should be able to use their knowledge of the properties of different types of fabric to suggest some different uses of fabrics.

● Most of the students should be able to describe and compare the properties of the different types of paper using a range of suitable property words they have learned in this topic. Circulate, making sure they are doing so correctly and asking questions to guide their thinking.

▲ Some of the students should be able to work collaboratively to predict the outcome of the investigation and ask and answer questions to complete the activity. Some students may struggle to decide how to test each of the properties, so you may need to write some outline steps on the board for them to follow.

Consolidation

Student's Book page 62

Chemistry learning objectives

- Use senses to explore and talk about different materials.
- Identify the characteristics of different materials.
- Recognise and name common materials.
- Sort objects into groups based on the properties of their materials.

Resources

- Workbook page 48
- Video C3: Sportspeople
- Assessment Sheets C1 and C2

Classroom equipment

- paper, scissors, glue
- selection of pre-cut fabrics
- example(s) of sports equipment

Looking back

- Use the summary points on Student's Book page 62 to review the key things that the students have learned in the topic. Ask questions such as: *In what ways can our senses help us find out more about materials? What can each sense tell us about a material? How many different materials can you name? In what ways are the properties of metal similar to wood? In what ways are they different? Can you name some different uses of plastic and paper? What two ways can we use to sort objects into groups?*

- Show the class Video C3, which shows people taking part in different sports. Discuss the different objects and different materials shown. If possible, have some examples of specialist sports equipment available for the students to examine. Then ask the students to complete the activity on Workbook page 48. They should think of all the properties needed for particular objects and suggest some materials that might be suitable for them. Ask questions such as: *Which equipment needs the most flexibility? Which needs the least?* Finish by reviewing that materials are chosen to suit the purpose of the object they are used for. This activity will show you how well the students have understood the topic.

How well do you remember?

You may use the revision and consolidation activities on Student's Book page 62, either as a test or as a paired class activity. If you are using the activities as a test, have the students work on their own to complete the tasks in writing, and then collect and mark the work. If you are using them as a class activity, you may prefer to let the students do the tasks orally.

Circulate as they discuss the questions and observe the students carefully to see who is confident and who is unsure of the concepts.

Some suggested answers

1 Students' own collages.
2 Wood: trees, table, bench, stool, paper napkins, newspaper, basket; fabric: clothes, table cloth, basket cover, hair ribbons; glass: glasses, jug; plastics: glasses, jug, plates, ball; metal: forks; stone: rocks; combined materials: digital camera.
3 Cricket bat: hard and strong, wood; tennis ball: light and flexible, fabric or plastic; weights: heavy and strong, metal; trainers: light and flexible, plastic, fabric or leather.

Assessment

A more formal assessment of the students' understanding of the topic can be undertaken using Assessment Sheets C1 and C2. This can be completed in class or as a homework task.

Students following Cambridge Primary Science Framework will write progression tests set and supplied by Cambridge Assessment International Education at this level and feedback will be given regarding their achievement levels.

Assessment Sheet answers

Sheet C1
1 Students' own answers. [10]

Sheet C2
1 Students' own answers. [2]
2 Students' own answers. [2]
3 shirt, sponge [2]
4 see-through, smooth, easy to clean [3]
5 True [1]

Student's Book answers

Pages 48–49

1 Students' own answers.
2 Students' own answers.
3 Students' own answers.
4 Students' own answers.
5 No, we can touch it, listen to it, taste it and smell it.

Pages 50–51

1 The glass is see-through. The brush is soft, the pot is hard but not as hard as the glass. The pot is orange the brush is brown, etc.
2 The stone for the pavement.
3 To provide a firm and hard-wearing surface.
4 No. The bottom has split, the bag is not strong enough to carry the shopping.

Pages 52–53

1 Students' own answers.
2 Answers might include: shop windows, car windscreens, sunglasses, car headlights.
3 So it can be stored easily, so it can be tied around things easily, etc.
4 Students' own answers.
5 Waterproof does not let water in. Absorbent does let water in.

Pages 54–55

1 For wood, answers might include: wardrobe, chair, bed, bedside cupboard. For plastic, answers might include: toys, clock.
2 Answers might include: duvet cover, pillow, cushion, clothes, teddy bears, carpet, etc.
3 For metal, answers might include: car, bus, umbrella frame, bicycle, motorbike, lamp post, etc. For glass, answers might include: windows, car windscreen, bus windows.
4 Answers might include: umbrella, raincoat, car, bus, house, etc.
5 They are strong, hard wearing and waterproof.

Pages 56–57

1 Students' own answers.
2 Plastic, glass, metal – they are strong and hard wearing.
3 Plastic, fabric.
4 Answers might include: lightweight, cheap, keeps the food warm/cool.
5 Because some objects are very big and if their materials were too heavy they might collapse or be difficult to use.

Pages 58–59

1 Answers might include: fabric, wood, glass, metal, water, paper, etc.
2 Goldfish bowl, mirror, window.
3 Desk, books, etc.
4 Students' own answers.
5 Students' own answers.

Pages 60–61

1 Wool, silk, cotton.
2 Students' own answers.
3 Answers might include: lightweight, see-through, strong, soft, easy to mould, etc.
4 It is lightweight, flexible, cheap, strong, easy to mould, etc.
5 Students' own answers.

4.1 Movement

Scientific background

Animals and plants are *living things*. All living things carry out the seven life processes, though they do so in very different ways: they *move*, *respire*, *grow*, *reproduce* (have young), *feed*, *excrete* waste and are *sensitive* to changes in their environment (via their senses). Students learned about growth, having young and senses in earlier topics. In this unit, they will look at the different types of movement of familiar things, both living and non-living.

Animals' movements depend on the shapes and sizes of their bodies (legs, wings, fins) and where they live (land, water or both). Animals' movements can also depend on how they get their food, reproduce and protect themselves.

The human body is adapted to stand erect, to walk on two feet and to use the arms to carry and lift. Humans are capable of a wide range of movements, from walking to swimming to jumping.

Non-living things cannot move by themselves. A force needs to be applied to cause the movement and the force can also determine the type of movement, for example whether a ball rolls or spins. Students will learn about pushing and pulling forces later in this topic.

Introduction

- Use the topic opener photograph on Student's Book page 63 as a talking point. Ask the students to describe what they can see. Tell them that they are going to look at some different types of movement and learn about some types of forces.

- Recap what the students learned in Topic 1 by asking: *What can humans and animals do? Why do animals need to move?* (to find food and water, to find shelter and to stay safe from predators)

- Write *move* on the board and introduce the second key word: *movement*. Jump up and down on the spot a few times. Ask: *What am I doing?* Explain that jumping is a type of movement.

Teaching and learning activities

- Ask the class to look at the pictures on Student's Book page 64. Ask them to discuss their answers in groups, then take feedback as a class, encouraging them to try to use as many different movement words as possible. Write a class list on the board. Elicit words such as *run*, *spin*, *swing*, *jump*, *swim*, etc.

- Show the class Slideshow P1, of different animals moving. After the slideshow, allow the students to talk about what they have seen. Ask: *Which animals move slowly? Which move quickly? Which animals swim? Which animals crawl?* Introduce more movement words as necessary, such as *slither*, and add these to the list on the board. Play the slideshow again, pausing after each picture. Invite the students to mimic how the animal moves.

- Lay out a set of cards cut from PCM P1. Ask a student to pick up a card, to show it to you and then role-play the animal. The rest of the class must try to identify the animal. When all the cards have been used, ask the class to sort them into groups based on the different ways that the animals move. Establish that all animals can move but they do so in different ways.

● Ask the students to stand, spaced well apart. Say: *Show me how many different ways you can move.* Let them hop, jump, wave their arms to show you. Ask: *Which parts of your body were you using? Do people move in the same way as animals? Do young animals move in the same way as their parents?* Let the students explain their ideas, and ask and answer questions with other students.

● Show the class Slideshow P2, of different construction machines and vehicles. Write *lifting, tipping, digging, pushing, mixing, turning, moving forwards* and *moving backwards* on the board. Pause the slideshow after each picture and ask the students to describe the movements of the machine or vehicle using these words.

● Make sure the students understand the questions on Student's Book page 65. Ask them to discuss their answers in groups, then take feedback.

Graded activities

1 Show the class Video P1, of different animals moving. Play the video once and then play it again, pausing after each animal. Ask the students to work with a partner to describe how each animal moves. Ask: *Which animals move slowly? Which move quickly? Which animals run? Which animals jump? Which animals can move in more than one way? Which ways can they move?* Add any new movement words to the list on the board.

2 Give each pair of students a large sheet of paper, some pictures of animals and some glue. Ask them to sort the pictures into groups based on the ways that the different animals move. They should then divide their paper into different sections, one for each movement type (swim, crawl, walk, etc.) and stick the pictures to make a poster. Circulate to make sure they have grouped the animals correctly before they glue them onto the paper.

3 Talk to the students about the animals that live in the environment around your school, e.g. humans, birds, insects. Ask them to name as many as they can. Remind them to think about those that live in trees or in water, as well as those on land. Then take the class on a walk around the school

grounds. Tell them to do a survey of the different ways they see animals moving. They should record their findings on Workbook page 49. Ask: *Do animals have only one way of moving? Can a bird move in more than one way?* Discuss how to classify animals such as birds (walk or fly or both?) and agree a consistent way to record their movement. Depending on ability, the students can display their results as a bar chart. Explain that this is a useful method for recording data.

Consolidate and review

● Use Workbook page 50 to consolidate the teaching and to check the students can identify things that move in different ways.

Differentiation

■ All of the students should be able to recognise some of the familiar ways in which the animals move and name the different types of movement, such as *run* and *swim*. More able students should be able to identify some of the less familiar types of movement, such as *slither*.

● Most of the students should be able to sort a selection of animal pictures into groups based on type of movement. Circulate, reminding students that some animals will be able to fit into more than one group as they can move in more than one way.

▲ Some of the students should be able to follow instructions and accurately record data using first-hand observations. Recording their findings in tabular form and then converting them into a bar chart are both useful exercises for practising a method for recording data.

Big Cat 🐾

Students who have read *Big Cat I can do it* will notice the different ways that animals move, and will see how children copy these movements.

4.2 Pushing and pulling

Student's Book pages 66–67

Physics learning objective
- Recognise that both pushes and pulls are forces.

Resources
- Workbook pages 51 and 52
- PCM P2: Pushing and pulling

Classroom equipment
- cardboard box
- some heavy objects, such as books

- selection of toys that work by pushing or pulling
- wooden or plastic building block (or similar)
- toy car with string attached for pulling it
- coloured pens or pencils

Scientific enquiry skills
- *Ideas and evidence:* Try to answer questions by collecting evidence through observation.

Key words
- force
- push
- pull

Scientific background

For an object to move, there needs to be a *force* acting on it. A *force* can most simply be described as a *push* or a *pull*. Squeezing, stretching and twisting are also types of forces, but the students will not be introduced to these at this stage. Forces cannot be seen but they can be felt. The students will need the opportunity to try out pushing and pulling for themselves to fully understand the concept. The effects of forces can be seen in the resulting motion: the students will see what happens to toys when they are pushed or pulled.

Pushing and pulling are basic ways of making things move. Even when we are using complicated devices, at the simplest level the devices work by pushing or pulling actions. Gears in machines or cars work by pushing, and trucks and trailers work by pulling. Railway systems work by pulling, as all the trucks or carriages are joined to each other and are pulled by the railway locomotive. Force should not be confused with energy or power, both concepts that will introduced in later stages.

Introduction

- Ask two students to come to the front of the class. Ask one student to push gently on the other student. Ask the student who was pushed to push back gently on the first student. Ask the class: *What has just happened?* Take answers and discuss students' ideas.

- Ask another pair of students to the front and tell one of the pair to pull the other gently. Ask the students: *Can you describe how this is different from what the other two students were doing?* Take students' answers and discuss what they mean.

- Ask all of the students to stand in pairs. Say that, when instructed, one of them should gently push the other. Then the same student in each pair should gently pull the other. Repeat the process, but change the active member of the pair. The purpose of this activity is to set the scene for the unit.

- Introduce and discuss the key words: *force*, *push*, *pull*. Write them on the board and point out how each word is spelled and pronounced. They will probably be familiar with the words *push* and *pull* from everyday use, but *force* is likely to be new to them. Tell the class that they are now going to find out more about pushes and pulls and what a force is.

Teaching and learning activities

- Start with a wooden or plastic building brick. Ask: *Can we make this brick move? What must we do to it?* Encourage the idea of pushing the brick as well as picking it up, throwing it, dropping it, etc. Replace the brick with a toy car with a piece of string attached to it. Ask: *What can we do to make this move?* Encourage the students to think about pulling the car.

- Ask the class to look at the pictures on Student's Book page 66. Ask: *How is the boy making the ball and the car move?* Establish that pushes and pulls are types of forces and that a force can make something move.

- Ask the students to look around them and to think of things in the classroom that they regularly move by pushing (e.g. the door, the light switch, etc.) and by pulling (e.g. the door, drawers, etc.). If necessary, demonstrate one of each type. Ask the students to work in groups to make a list. Share the students' ideas and make a class list on the board. Encourage all the students to use the words *push* and *pull* when they describe the actions.

- Further discuss how we push and pull things. For example, we push a wheelbarrow, a baby's pram and a vacuum cleaner but we pull suitcases on wheels, some toys. Invite the students to try pushing, and then pulling, a heavy box of books across the floor. Ask: *Which is easier, pushing or pulling?*

- Give each group a selection of toys. Encourage the students to make each toy work, and then to sort the toys into those that need a push and those that need a pull. You could provide two hoops or some large circles drawn onto paper to help with the sorting. Ask: *Were there any toys that were difficult to sort?*

- Ask the students to mime various activities, such as opening a door, pulling a rope, kicking a ball, riding a bike, while the other students watch. Ask: *What kind of action did you use, a push or a pull?*

- Make sure the students understand the questions on Student's Book pages 66–67. Establish that some things will work with either a push or a pull, and that we usually use our hands and arms to push and pull things.

Graded activities

1 Ask the students to complete the activity on Workbook page 51. Tell them that they should look at each object or action and decide whether it involves a push or a pull. They should then colour all the pictures which show a push. Circulate, asking questions as necessary to guide them: *What does the boy do to make the toy truck move? What do his hands do on the handle? Does the truck move away from him or towards him? What do we call the force that makes an object move away from you?*

2 Ask the students to work in pairs. Tell them to choose an object that works by being pushed or pulled. They should think about what the object does and how it works. Allow each pair time to plan how they are going to mime the actions to show how their chosen object works. They should then perform the mime to the class. Ask the rest of the class to try and guess the object and whether they understood what actions were being mimed. Discuss each one as a class.

3 Give each student a copy of PCM P2. Ask them to think about toys that need to be pushed or pulled to make them work. Tell them to draw pictures of the toys that they have thought of. They should draw them in the spaces on PCM P2, in the left-hand column for push toys and in the right-hand column for pull toys. Circulate, looking at the pictures that students have drawn and asking them how each toy works. Clarify any misconceptions.

Consolidate and review

- Use Workbook page 52 to consolidate the teaching and to check that the students can describe the force you use to make one push toy and one pull toy work.

- Allow the students to work in groups to investigate how a cardboard box filled with heavy objects can be moved by pushing or pulling. They can then remove some of the objects and compare how easy the box is to push and to pull.

Differentiation

■ All of the students should be able to correctly identify the things that show a push, with little prompting. If any students do need some help, ask them to imagine what they need to do in each case and to think about whether the action is a push or a pull.

● Most of the students should be able to work collaboratively, sharing ideas and thinking creatively about how best to mime the actions to show a push or pull object. Remind them to exaggerate their actions so that it is clear what they are showing.

▲ Some of the students should be able to draw a reasonable representation of their chosen toys and then describe how each one works using the words *push*, *pull* and *force*. If some students struggle to do this independently, display the push and pull toys from earlier in the lesson and allow them to choose from this selection to complete the activity.

Students who read *Big Cat Pushing and pulling* will quickly recognise all the different ways there are of pushing and pulling things to make them move.

4.3 Pushes and pulls

Student's Book pages 68–69

Physics learning objective
• Recognise that both pushes and pulls are forces.

Resources
• Workbook pages 53 and 54
• Video P2: Waterfalls
• PCM P3: Making a waterwheel

Classroom equipment
• non-motorised model car
• pictures of windmills
• paper, pieces of expanded polystyrene, cocktail sticks, paper sails, troughs of water or access to sink
• coloured pens or pencils
• stiff cardboard (e.g. corrugated), plates to draw round, scissors, sticky tape, skewers, source of water (tap or syringe)
• selection of five balls of different masses and sizes (make sure that the students will be able to move them by blowing on them)
• chalk or tape, tape measure, hand-held fan (battery operated)

Scientific enquiry skills
• *Plan investigative work:* Ask questions and contribute to discussions about how to seek answers; make predictions; decide what to do to try to answer a science question.
• *Obtain and present evidence:* Explore and observe in order to collect evidence (measurements and observations) to answer questions; suggest ideas and follow instructions; record stages in work.
• *Consider evidence and approach:* Make comparisons; compare what happened with predictions.

Key words
• **force**   • **water**   • **wind**

⚠ Supervise the students when they use scissors and glue. Supervise the students carefully when they push cocktail sticks into polystyrene, and when they push skewers through their cardboard waterwheels. You may prefer to do these steps for them.

Scientific background

We use different types of *forces* every day. Pushes and pulls can help us to do useful jobs.

Water can push with a large force. The faster the water flows and the bigger the volume of water, the greater the pushing force and the more movement it can produce. The waterwheel is an example of humans using the pushing force of water to do a job.

Wind can also provide a pushing force on an object. The stronger the wind, the greater the pushing force and the more movement it can produce. At this stage the students have not been taught about gases. They may think that air is 'nothing'. It is important that the students feel the force of moving air for themselves so that they can understand this lesson. In the context of sailing boats, a bigger sail means that the force of the wind acts over a larger surface area, and this provides a greater overall force.

Introduction

● Take a toy car and put it on a table. Ask a student to come to the front and make the car go. Ask the class: *What did they do to make the car go? Did they push it or pull it?* Review the previous lesson and establish that pushes and pulls are examples of forces.

● Ask the class to look at the pictures on Student's Book page 68. Ask: *Where is pushing being shown? Where is pulling being shown?* Identify which pictures show pushes and which show pulls. Ensure that the students know the difference between the two actions. Explain that we can use these forces to do useful jobs and that they are now going to look at some examples.

Teaching and learning activities

● Show the class Video P2, of some waterfalls. Ask the students to describe what the water is doing. Discuss that the falling water produces a very large force. Tell the students that we can sometimes use the force of falling water to do useful jobs.

Ask the students to look at the picture of a waterwheel on Student's Book page 69. Ask: *What makes the waterwheel turn?* Explain that waterwheels were once built to use the force of water to do useful jobs such as grinding flour.

● Ask the students to copy your actions. Hold a hand up in front of your face, with the palm facing towards you. Blow gently on your hand. As the students blow on their hands, ask: *What do you feel?* Then hold a piece of paper in front of your face and ask the students to copy you again. Blow on the paper. As they blow on their paper, ask: *What happens when you blow on the paper?* Show the students some pictures of windmills. Ask: *What makes the sails turn? Where does the force come from to make the sails turn?*

● Now direct the students to look at the pictures of sailing boats on Student's Book page 69. Discuss what is making the boats move. If *wind* is given as the answer, ask individual students if they can improve on this by using some science words. An improved answer would be that the *force* of the *wind* is *pushing* on the sails. Make sure the students understand the question. Explain, in simple terms, that the boat with the bigger sail will move faster because more wind can push on it, creating a bigger force.

● Let the students make their own boats. Use a small piece of polystyrene for the boat, a cocktail stick for the mast and a piece of paper for the sail. Using a water trough or sink, the students test their boats by blowing gently and then harder. The students should describe what happens, using the words *blow*, *hard*, *gently*, *move*, *fast*, *slow*.

Graded activities

1 Ask the students to complete the activity on Workbook page 53. Ask: *Have you all shown the same answers? Were there any things that you could not identify? Which things needed pushing or pulling to make them work?* Ask the students to explain their answers.

2 Tell the class they are going to make a waterwheel that turns when water pushes on the paddles. Give each group a copy of PCM P3 and a range of materials. Read out and demonstrate the instructions, then offer help as necessary as the students construct their own waterwheels in groups. Test the waterwheels in front of the whole class. Encourage the students to make comments and suggestions. Ask them to consider their own waterwheels, and those of others, and suggest

ways of improving the waterwheels to make them work better. Ask: *What can we do to make the waterwheel turn faster? Why does this happen?* Discuss, in simple terms, that if the water flows faster or we use more water, the pushing force will be bigger and the wheel will move faster.

3 Tell the class that they are going to do an investigation to find out which ball can be moved the most easily by blowing on it. Show them the five different balls. Ask: *Which ball do you think will be the easiest to move by blowing? Which do you think will be the hardest to move by blowing?* Let the students make predictions on Workbook page 54. Then ask them to decide how they could test their predictions. Ask individuals from each group to report back to the class. Ask the whole class how they could make the test fair. (The same person blowing with the same strength, blowing from the same distance to the ball.) Challenge the students to test the balls and rank them in order of easiest to most difficult. For some groups provide chalk or tape to mark the distance travelled by each ball. Allow others to use a tape measure. Now demonstrate a fairer version of the test to the whole class. Use a hand-held battery-operated fan to provide a constant stream of air. Students should record their results on Workbook page 54.

Consolidate and review

● Ask the students to work in pairs to describe how a waterwheel and a windmill work. This will show how well they have understood the unit.

Differentiation

■ All of the students should be able to correctly identify the things that work by pushing or pulling.

● Most of the students should be able to work together to follow instructions to make their waterwheel with some support.

▲ Some of the students should be able to work collaboratively to make predictions about the outcome of the investigation, but some may need a little help to do this. Some of the students will be able to carry out the investigation independently, recording their results and asking and answering questions to clarify their thinking. If students are not at this level yet, you may prefer to do this as a teacher-led class investigation.

4.4 Faster or slower?

Student's Book pages 70–71

Physics learning objective

- Recognise that when things speed up, slow down or change direction there is a cause.

Resources

- Workbook pages 55, 56 and 57
- PCM P4: How far does it travel?

Classroom equipment

- sets of three identical toy cars
- several footballs
- chalk or other markers
- metre rules, tape measures or pieces of string
- large sheets of paper
- coloured pens or pencils

Scientific enquiry skills

- *Ideas and evidence:* Try to answer questions by collecting evidence through observation.

- *Plan investigative work:* Ask questions and contribute to discussions about how to seek answers; make predictions; decide what to do to try to answer a science question.
- *Obtain and present evidence:* Explore and observe in order to collect evidence (measurements and observations) to answer questions; suggest ideas and follow instructions; record stages in work.
- *Consider evidence and approach:* Make comparisons; compare what happened with predictions.

Key words

- **faster**
- **slower**
- **stop**

 Remind the students to be careful when they are rolling balls to each other and racing the toy cars.

Scientific background

Forces affect objects in different ways. This unit focuses on the idea that a force can make an object move *faster*, move *slower*, *start* to move, or *stop moving*. In most situations there are at least two forces acting on an object. If these forces are *balanced*, an object will not change its speed. Without friction or air resistance an object would keep moving at the same speed, without the need for any force. (This contrasts with our everyday experience, in which friction and air resistance act to slow down moving objects and we need to supply a force to maintain their speed.)

The initial speed of an object depends on the force exerted on it to make it start to move. For example, the faster or harder something is thrown, the greater the speed at which it travels. The mass of the object is also a factor. A larger force is also needed to stop a faster-moving object. Note that the students will often confuse the size of an object and the mass of an object. At this stage, they do not need to understand this level of detail; they are simply being introduced to the concept that a force can cause something to speed up, slow down, start to move, or stop moving.

Introduction

- Push a toy car to make it cross the classroom floor. Ask the students to talk to their partner about why it moves. If necessary, remind them that the car needs a force to move, and your hand gives the car that force when you push it.
- Ask the class to look at the pictures of the footballer on Student's Book page 70. Allow the students to briefly discuss what is happening in Picture A and then the same for Picture B. The purpose of this activity is to assess the students' existing knowledge, which can then be built upon in the rest of the unit. Tell them that they are now going to learn more about what forces can do.

Teaching and learning activities

- Push the toy car gently forwards in front of the class. Ask: *What did I do to make the car move?* Emphasise that the car moved because a force was applied in the form of a push. Use this to establish that a force can make an object start to move. Push the car again. This time, once the car is moving, push the car gently in the opposite direction to make it come to a stop. Ask: *What happened? Why did this happen?* Explain that a force can also stop an object from moving.

- Make sure the students understand the questions on Student's Book page 70. Establish that Picture A shows the ball starting to move and Picture B shows the ball coming to a stop. In both cases, it is because the footballer has applied a force to the ball.

- Provide each group of students with a football. They should roll the ball to each other at about the same speed. Ask: *What do you feel?* Then ask them to vary the speed of the ball. Ask: *Is it different? In what way is it different? If the ball is moving faster, do you need a bigger or smaller force to make it stop moving?* Ask the students to think about cars moving on a road. Ask: *What happens if a fast-moving vehicle hits another object?* (It will crash, with a large force.) Remind the students that everyone must be very careful when they cross a road.

- Give each group of students a toy car to experiment with. Ask them to push the car forwards. Ask: *What can you do to make the car move faster? What can you do to make the car move slower?* Allow them time to discuss the questions, then talk through their ideas. Explain that a force can make an object move faster or slower. Using a bigger pushing force will make the toy car move faster.

- Ask the class to look at the pictures on Student's Book page 71. Discuss the questions as a class.

Graded activities

1 Give each student a copy of PCM P4. Ask them to work in pairs to roll a football, gently at first and then more strongly Support the students by helping them to think of a simple way to record the distance each ball rolls, for example by using a chalk mark or other marker. Once they have a way of recording the distance, they should roll the ball first with a small force and then with a big force. Ask them to record their results by drawing pictures on PCM P4. Ask: *Which ball went further? Why do you think it went further?*

2 Give each group of three students an identical toy car each. Tell them that you would like one of them to give their car a small push, one to give a medium push and one to give a big push. Ask them to work in their groups to predict which car will move the fastest. They should then plan an investigation to find out if they are correct. Ask

the students to write their predictions and plan on Workbook pages 55–56. Encourage them to give reasons for their predictions. Refer them to the pictures on Student's Book page 71 for ideas.

3 Set up a straight race track for the toy cars. Mark a start line and a finishing line, about a metre away from it. Explain to the students that their cars must start completely behind the start line and that they can only give their car one push. Ask the groups to carry out their investigation to find out which car moves the fastest. Remind the first student to push their car with a small force, the second student to use a medium force and the third student to use a big force. Students should see which car moves the fastest and then measure the distances travelled. Show them how to use metre rules or pieces of string. Ask the students to record and explain their results on Workbook pages 56–57, and then compare them with their predictions. Ask them about the results and what they show. Discuss their findings as a class.

Consolidate and review

- Give each group a large sheet of paper and some coloured pens. Ask them to design a safety poster for crossing the road. It should warn children that moving traffic is dangerous. Explain that this is because it is difficult for vehicles to stop suddenly.

Differentiation

■ All of the students should be able to describe the differences between the two forces and draw reasonable representations of their results, with just a little help.

● Most of the students should be able to work together, asking and answering questions to clarify their thinking and to predict the outcome of the investigation. Most should be able to explain their reasoning.

▲ Some of the students should be able to work collaboratively and support each other in order to follow instructions and carry out the investigation. Some of the students should be able to accurately record their results in tabular form. If the students are not at this level yet, you may prefer to do this as a teacher-led class investigation.

4.5 Changing direction

Student's Book pages 72–73

Physics learning objective

- Recognise that when things speed up, slow down or change direction there is a cause.

Resources

- Workbook pages 58 and 59
- Video P3: Kicking a ball
- Video P4: Playing snooker
- Video P5: Footballers
- PCM P5: Toy bumping

Classroom equipment

- variety of different sized and shaped balls (e.g. ping pong ball, tennis ball, cricket ball, football, rugby ball, beach ball, golf ball, squash ball, marble, ball bearing), chalk for marking lines and goals
- drinking straws, table-tennis balls
- sets of two different balls

Scientific enquiry skills

- *Ideas and evidence:* Try to answer questions by collecting evidence through observation.
- *Plan investigative work:* Ask questions and contribute to discussions about how to seek answers; make predictions; decide what to do to try to answer a science question.
- *Obtain and present evidence:* Explore and observe in order to collect evidence (measurements and observations) to answer questions; suggest ideas and follow instructions; record stages in work.
- *Consider evidence and approach:* Make comparisons; compare what happened with predictions.

Key word

- **direction**

⚠️ Students should conduct their outdoor investigation under careful supervision. Remind them to be careful when they are rolling balls to each other.

Scientific background

Forces affect objects in different ways. Forces can make an object start to move or speed up, they can stop an object or make it slow down and they can also change the direction of an object. This is very important in physics and is why the Moon orbits the Earth. The pull of gravity changes the Moon's direction and stops it from travelling in a straight line out into space. This unit introduces the students to the idea that a force can make an object *change direction*. The students will understand the concept better with everyday examples, for example, a footballer changing the direction of the ball to shoot at goal.

In all ball games, the players exert a force on the ball by striking it with part of their body, a racket or a club. Part of the skill in these games is to apply the right amount of force in just the right direction, often at just the right time. Many activities require the athlete to apply the maximum force possible, for example, to a shot, javelin, hammer or weights.

Introduction

- Review the previous unit by asking the students what happened to the two footballs on Student's Book page 70. Ask: *What happened when the footballer touched the ball?* Take feedback and elicit that a force can make an object start to move and make an object stop moving. Reinforce this by showing the class Video P3, of a ball being kicked in slow motion, to illustrate a pushing force making a ball start to move. Extend the discussion to recap that a force can also make an object move faster or slower. Tell the class that they are now going to learn about something else a force can do to an object.

- Ask the students to look at the pictures on Student's Book page 72. Discuss the pictures and then answer the questions as a class. Talk through the students' ideas first and then introduce the idea that a force can change the direction of a moving object.

Teaching and learning activities

- Show the students a ball and ask: *What words can you use to describe what this ball looks like?*

Give each group a ball and ask: *What does the ball feel like? What are some ways that the ball can move? Can you name some games that use each type of movement?* Allow them time to discuss the questions in their groups and then talk through the students' ideas as a class.

● Take the students outside and provide a variety of balls of different sizes. Mark out a distance on the ground and have the students roll each ball as near as possible to the far line. Ask: *Which is easiest to roll? Which is hardest? Which rolled the fastest? Which rolled the slowest?* Allow them time to test this. Place a ball on the floor. Hold a second ball. Ask: *What will happen if I roll this ball and it hits the ball on the floor?* The students should realise that the rolling ball will make the other ball start to move.

● Back in the classroom, show the class Video P4, of snooker being played. Discuss what the students can see, and elicit that the cue ball pushes on the other balls, making them start to move and causing the moving cue ball to change direction.

● Make sure the students understand the questions on Student's Book page 73. Ask them to discuss their answers in groups, then take feedback as a class.

● Tell the class they are going to play a game of blow football, where straws are used to blow a table-tennis ball. Each player tries to blow the ball into their opponent's goal. After they have been playing for about 5 minutes, ask: *Was it easy to make the ball go where you wanted it to? What did you do to make the ball move? What did you do to make the ball change direction? Did you need to blow hard? What happened if you blew very hard?* Let them discuss these questions in the groups and ask them to explain their answers. Conclude that blowing pushed the balls and that this force could make the balls start to move, move faster and change direction.

Graded activities

1 Show the class Video P5, of footballers. Ask: *What are the footballers using their force to do? What happens to the ball when they kick it?* Ask the students to discuss this in their groups. Then invite them to feedback as a class and explain the reasoning for their answers.

2 Give each group of students two different balls. Tell them that you would like them to roll the balls towards each other so that they collide. Ask them to work in their groups to predict what will

happen. They should then plan an investigation to find out if they are correct. Ask the students to write their predictions and plan on Workbook page 58. Encourage them to give reasons for their predictions. Ask questions to guide their thinking if they need some help: *What will happen to the balls? Will they stop moving? Will they slow down or move faster? Will they change direction?*

3 You may need a big space for this activity. Ask the groups to carry out their investigation to find out what happens when they roll the two balls towards each other and they collide. Ask the students to record and explain their results on Workbook page 59, and then compare them with their predictions. Ask them about the results and what they show. Ask: *Which happened to each ball? Did it move faster? Did it slow down? Did it change direction? Did it stop moving?* Give the groups a few minutes to discuss their results, then discuss their findings as a class.

Consolidate and review

● Use PCM P5 to consolidate the teaching and to check that the students can describe what happens when one toy vehicle rolls into another. This activity will show how well the students have understood the unit.

Differentiation

■ All of the students should be able to apply their acquired knowledge to discuss the effects that the footballers have on the balls.

● Most of the students should be able to work together, asking and answering questions to clarify their thinking and to predict the outcome of the investigation. Most of the students should be able to explain their reasoning, with some support, demonstrating that they have understood the work in this unit.

▲ Some of the students should be able to work collaboratively and support each other in order to follow instructions and carry out the investigation. Some of the students should be able to accurately record their results and then compare the results with their predictions. If students are not at this level yet, you may prefer to do this as a teacher-led class investigation.

Consolidation

Student's Book page 74
Physics learning objectives
- Explore, talk about and describe the movement of familiar things.
- Recognise that both pushes and pulls are forces.
- Recognise that when things speed up, slow down or change direction there is a cause.

Resources
- Workbook page 60
- Assessment Sheets P1 and P2

Looking back

- Use the summary points on Student's Book page 74 to review the key things that the students have learned in the topic. Ask questions such as: *How many different ways can you move? Which parts of your body do you use for each movement? Do people move in the same ways as animals? How many different ways can we make a ball move? What kind of action do you use in each case, a push or a pull? What makes a waterwheel turn? What can make a waterwheel turn faster? Why? What does it feel like when you catch a ball that was thrown gently? What does it feel like if the ball was thrown hard?* Encourage the students to use the word *force* in their answers.

- Ask the students to complete the activity on Workbook page 60. They should make a list of some different ball games and say how you make the ball move in each game. Circulate, asking: *What does the ball do? What makes the ball do this? Does the ball move faster? Does the ball change direction? Do you need to use a big force or a small force?* This activity will show you how well the students have understood the topic.

How well do you remember?

You may use the revision and consolidation activities on Student's Book page 74, either as a test or as a paired class activity. If you are using the activities as a test, have the students work on their own to complete the tasks in writing, and then collect and mark the work. If you are using them as a class activity, you may prefer to let the students do the tasks orally. Circulate as they discuss the questions and observe the students carefully to see who is confident and who is unsure of the concepts.

Some suggested answers

1 Two pushes: the wind blowing the kite, and the boys kicking the ball.
2 The ball might move faster, the ball might direction.
3 Students' own answers, e.g. basketball: bounce, throw; tennis: throw, hit; golf: hit; rugby: throw, kick; badminton: throw, hit

Assessment

A more formal assessment of the students' understanding of the topic can be undertaken using Assessment Sheets P1 and P2. This can be completed in class or as a homework task.

Students following Cambridge Primary Science Framework will write progression tests set and supplied by Cambridge Assessment International Education at this level and feedback will be given regarding their achievement levels.

Assessment Sheet answers

Sheet P1
1 swims – fish, walks – camel, flies – bird, slithers – snake [4]
2 bird and worm, car and trailer [2]
3 pushes, direction [2]
4 push, force [2]

Sheet P2
1 The pull-along giraffe. [1]
2 C [1], A [1], It would not move. [1]
3 False, false [2]
4 Students' own answers. [2]
5 It slows down or changes direction. [2]

Student's Book answers

Pages 64–65

1 Answers might include: animals, orangutan hanging from a tree, orcas swimming, deer running/jumping, boy rolling a snowball, horse running, etc.

2 Answers might include: swinging, swimming, running, jumping, rolling, etc.

3 Sitting, running, swimming, catching a ball (playing).

4 Answers might include: jump, skip, run, walk, crawl, climb, shake, swim, etc.

5 Answers might include: flying, walking, climbing, etc.

Pages 66–67

1 He is pushing it.

2 He is pulling it.

3 Push: trolley, tricycle. Pull: giraffe.

4 Yes: you can push or pull the trolley, tricycle and giraffe.

5 Your hands/arms.

Pages 68–69

1 You pull the plug out. You push the shopping trolley.

2 Push: camera button, car. Pull: fishing net, cart.

3 The water pushing down on it.

4 The wind pushing the sails.

5 The blue boat. It has a bigger sail so there is a greater force pushing it.

Pages 70–71

1 Footballer A.

2 Footballer B.

3 Because the footballer catches the ball and stops it from moving.

4 They are going to push their cars and have a race.

5 The green car.

6 It had the biggest force./It was pushed with the most force.

Pages 72–73

1 The footballer is heading the ball. He is pushing it with his head.

2 It makes the ball change direction.

3 The cricketer is hitting the ball with his bat.

4 He uses a push.

5.1 **Listen carefully**

Student's Book pages 76–77

Physics learning objective

• Identify many sources of sound.

Resources

• Workbook pages 61 and 62
• PCM P6: Sound source survey

Classroom equipment

• small bell
• plain paper or notebooks
• coloured pens or pencils
• six identical glass bottles filled with different amounts of water

Scientific enquiry skills

• *Ideas and evidence:* Try to answer questions by collecting evidence through observation.

Key words

• **sound**   • **source**

⚠ If you take the students on a walk around the school grounds, ensure they are safe and that they stay together. Be aware of any students who may have a hearing impairment, and adapt the lesson accordingly.

Scientific background

A sound is made when something moves backwards and forwards very quickly. We usually call this *vibrating*. The scientific term for it is *oscillating*. The *frequency* of sound is measured in Hertz (Hz). A musician would call a note with a frequency of 40Hz a *low* note. A note with a frequency of 90Hz would be called a *high* note.

If you blow across the top of a bottle you can hear a note. The less liquid there is in the bottle, the lower the note will be; it is the air inside the bottle, that is oscillating. If you want to make a louder sound you have to put in more effort, e.g. by hitting a drum skin harder. By putting in more effort into plucking a string or hitting a drum, you make the size of the oscillations bigger. This is called the *amplitude*. So a loud sound is made by an oscillation with a large amplitude. Different instruments have different *sound qualities*. This is known as the *tone* of the instrument.

At this stage, the students will be learning about and identifying different sources of sound; they do not need to understand how a sound is made. This will be covered in more detail in Stage 4 of this course.

Introduction

● Use the topic opener photograph on Student's Book page 75 as a talking point. Ask the students to describe what they can see (a band). Remind the students about their five senses, which they learned in Topic 2, and ask them to name each sense and

the sense organ associated with it. Introduce the key word *sound* and elicit that sounds are heard when they enter the ear. Ask the students to imagine what sounds they would hear if they were listening to the band in the picture. Tell them that they are going to learn all about sound in this topic.

● Ask the students to look at the top picture on Student's Book page 76, and discuss question 1 as a class. Next, let the students look at the bottom picture and discuss questions 2 and 3 in small groups. After a few minutes, take feedback from the groups and see if they all identified the same things that do not make sounds.

● Introduce the key word *source*. Invite the students to suggest what this might mean. Ascertain that the source of a sound is where it comes from. This will help you assess their prior knowledge of the subject.

Teaching and learning activities

● Ring a small bell. Ask the class: *Can you tell me how you knew that the bell rang?* Take some responses. Ask: *What part of your body are you using to listen? Where are your ears? What other sounds do you hear with your ears?* Take some responses.

● Form two equal groups. Number the students in each group, so that everyone has a partner. Match each number to an animal, for example, the number ones are cats, the number twos are goats.

The students must keep their number and animal secret. When you say: *Start!* they must make the sound of their animal and try to find their partner, based on hearing the animal sounds. The game ends when all the students have found their partners. Take feedback, asking: *What did you have to do to find your partner? Was it easy? Why?*

● Arrange six identical glass bottles in a line, with different amounts of water in each. Show the students how to blow across the top of a bottle to make a sound. Let the students blow across the tops and describe the sounds. They should then try tapping the bottles with a pencil. Ask: *Do all the bottles produce the same sound? Can you describe the sounds? Are the sounds the same when you tap the bottles and when you blow over them?* Let the students discuss the answers. Accept any reasonable descriptions. You could write a list of the descriptive words on the board.

Graded activities

1 Ask the students to turn to Workbook page 61 and to look at the activity. Make sure the students understand the words *bang*, *buzz*, *click*, *hiss* and *splash* before they begin. Ask the students to complete the activity on their own. Circulate and help any students that are having difficulty matching the sounds to the sources of the sound.

2 Ask the students to sit quietly in the classroom. Ask: *How many different sounds can you hear? What is the source of each sound?* Encourage them to make a list (by writing or drawing) and to classify the sounds as being either natural or human-made. Ask: *Why do you think this?* Let the students share their answers and write a list on the board of all the sounds they heard. Identify and discuss any differences the students may have observed when identifying a sound as being either natural or human-made.

3 Divide the students into groups of four or five. Take them for a walk around the school grounds to listen for different sounds. They can use copies of PCM P6 to record the sounds that they hear and their sources, or they can write their own lists in their notebooks. Encourage the students to use a variety of descriptive sound words, either in English or in their own language, for example rumbling, whistling, rushing, pattering, crashing. Once back inside the classroom, ask the students to draw a map of the school grounds (or to copy

a map of the grounds you have sketched on the board). They should mark on the map the place where they heard each sound and add a label to say what the source of the sound was, for example whistling/tweeting – bird, rumbling – a car/truck, and also to say if the sound was natural or human-made.

Consolidate and review

● Use Workbook page 62 to consolidate the teaching. Make sure the students understand the words *beep*, *bang* and *click*, before they begin.

● Let the students work in pairs, at opposite ends of a long table. Ask one student to put their head on the table, with their ear pressed against it. Ask the other to tap the table very gently. The first student should count how many times the second student taps the table. Let them swap roles.

Differentiation

■ Some of the students will need help reading the words and matching them to the pictures. More able students may like to suggest some alternative descriptive words that could be used.

● Most of the students should be able to write the different sounds they can hear.

▲ Some of the students will confidently create their own lists of sounds and sources of sounds without needing to use PCM P6. They will be able to accurately copy a map of the school grounds from the board and add locations and labels with little or no help.

5.2 What made that sound?

Student's Book pages 78–79

Physics learning objective

• Identify many sources of sound.

Resources

• Workbook page 63
• PCM P7: Musical instruments
• PCM P8: Sound word cards
• PCM P9: Blow, pluck or strike?
• Audio clip P1: Sounds familiar
• Audio clip P2: What is it?
• Video P6: Music

Classroom equipment

• a selection of different musical instruments for students to explore, if possible (or pictures of musical instruments): include strings, wind and percussion

Scientific enquiry skills

• *Ideas and evidence:* Try to answer questions by collecting evidence through observation.
• *Plan investigative work:* Make predictions.
• *Obtain and present evidence:* Explore and observe in order to collect evidence (measurements and observations) to answer questions.
• *Consider evidence and approach:* Make comparisons; compare what happened with predictions.

Key words

• **sound**   • **source**

⚠ Be aware of any students who may have a hearing impairment, and adapt the lesson accordingly.

Scientific background

Sound is made by vibrations that travel through the air to our ears. Stringed instruments make a sound when their strings are plucked or strummed because the strings vibrate, and the vibrations are transferred to the air. The sound of a wind instrument comes when we blow air into it, causing the air inside to vibrate. Percussion instruments vibrate when they are struck. The human voice is made by breathing air over our vocal cords, causing them to vibrate; it is like a cross between a stringed and a wind instrument.

Musical instruments work by amplifying vibrations. The body of the instrument resonates and amplifies the noise, making it louder.

At this stage, the students will be learning about, and identifying, different sources of sound; they do not need to understand how a sound is made. This will be covered in more detail in Stage 4 of this course.

Introduction

● Remind the students about the sounds they heard in previous lesson. Ask them to sort the sounds into two groups, guiding them to say natural sounds and human-made sounds. Ask the students to look at the pictures on Student's Book pages 78–79. Elicit that natural sounds can be made by the wind

or rain. Discuss how humans and animals can make sounds, asking: *How many different ways can you think of that humans make sounds?* (speaking, singing, moving, etc.)

● Ask the students: *Do you know anyone who plays a musical instrument? What kind of instrument is it? Can you describe how it makes sounds?* Show the students Video P6, then ask them to describe and explain how each instrument is played.

● Return to Student's Book pages 78–79 and answer questions 1–3 as a class. Elicit that musical instruments can be plucked, blown into or struck in order to produce a sound. Let the students answer questions 4 and 5 in their groups.

Teaching and learning activities

● Give the students copies of PCM P7 and ask them to draw a line to match each musical instrument with the action that is required to produce a sound.

● Hand out a set of word cards cut from PCM P8 to each group. Read each word with the class, asking them to repeat it after you and making sure the students understand what each word means. Say the name of a musical instrument out loud, either in English or in the students' own language (you could also show pictures of the different instruments). The students should hold up the correct word card to match the way that instrument is played.

Graded activities

1 Ask the students to look at the picture on Workbook page 63. They should circle all of the sound sources. Let them swap books with a partner and look to see if they have circled the same sources. Still in pairs, ask the students to act out a sound from the picture and let their partner point to the source of the sound. Come together as a class and ask the students to say some words that describe the sounds in the picture, for example *loud*, *soft*, *noisy*, *quiet*. Write these on the board. Tell the students they will be learning more about loud and soft sounds later on in this topic.

2 Tell the students that they must sit very quietly and listen to some sounds. Play Audio clip P1 of some familiar sounds, all the way through. Repeat the audio clip, but this time ask the students to name the source of each sound. Go through the answers with the class, identifying each source of sound. (1. Applause, 2. Bell, 3. Rooster crowing, 4. Thunder, 5. Water boiling, 6. Walking on gravel) Ask the students to say where they might hear each sound. Ask: *Is this a natural sound or a human-made sound?*

3 Give groups of students three different musical instruments to explore (each group should have a wind, string and percussion instrument). Ask them to predict what sound each one will make. They should then use the instrument to make a sound. Ask: *Was the sound the same as you predicted? If not, why not?* As a whole class, ask the students to sort the musical instruments into three groups. Lead the students to sort them into wind, string and percussion. You can use copies of PCM P9 to help guide students. Ask: *Why have you chosen these groups?* (blow, pluck, strike/hit) *Can any of the instruments be put into more than one group? Can the groups be sorted into smaller groups?* (for example, drums, bells, shakers) Ask individual students to demonstrate how each instrument works by blowing, plucking or striking it.

Consolidate and review

● Play Audio clip P2 of some unfamiliar sounds (1. Bubbles underwater, 2. Sawing wood, 3. Camera taking photos with film, 4. Helicopter, 5. A sheet of glass smashing, 6. Human heart beat). Ask the students to identify the sound sources. Help them as necessary by acting out some clues.

● Play a game of 'I can hear with my little ear, something that sounds like ...'. The students should name the source of the sound.

● Review the day's lesson. Ask the class the following questions and discuss their responses.
   ◆ *In today's lesson what did you hear?*
   ◆ *What did you use to hear these things?*
   ◆ *Was it difficult to name the sounds from the audio clips?*
   ◆ *Can you describe the sounds in detail? Use as many describing words as you can.*

Differentiation

■ All of the students should be able to circle the sources of sounds. They will be able to use some descriptive words to describe the sounds, including *loud* and *soft*, and understand what they mean.

● Most of the students should be able to identify and correctly name the sources of the sounds from the audio clip, with little prompting. Most students should be able to say if they are natural or human-made, although less able students may need some additional guidance.

▲ Some of the students will correctly predict what sound each musical instrument will make. They will be able to confidently sort them into three groups and suggest ways of sorting them into even more groups. More able students may begin to make the connection between sound and the vibration of a musical instrument. Most of the students will be able to correctly sort the instruments into three groups using PCM P9 as a guide. Less able students may need some prompting in order to predict the sounds each instrument will make and to sort them into three groups.

5.3 Hearing sounds

Student's Book pages 80–81

Physics learning objective

• Know that we hear when sound enters our ear.

Resources

• Workbook page 64
• Audio clip P1: Sounds familiar
• Audio clip P2: What is it?
• PCM P10: Different sounds

Classroom equipment

• ear defenders
• wooden spoons or drumsticks
• a selection of objects for students to strike to make a sound (for example plastic bottle, glass jar, drum, tennis ball, woollen pullover, metal spoon, etc)
• large sheets of paper, scissors, glue, coloured pens or pencils
• old magazines and pictures

Scientific enquiry skills

• *Ideas and evidence:* Try to answer questions by collecting evidence through observation.
• *Plan investigative work*: Make predictions.
• *Obtain and present evidence*: Explore and observe in order to collect evidence (measurements and observations) to answer questions.
• *Consider evidence and approach*: Compare what happened with predictions.

Key words

• **sound**
• **sense organ**

> ⚠ Be aware of any students who may have a hearing impairment, and adapt the lesson accordingly. Supervise the students when they use scissors and glue.

Scientific background

There are three parts to the ear. Sound waves travel through the air and into the outer ears. The sound waves move along a short tunnel until they reach a thin layer of skin, called the *eardrum*, which vibrates. In the middle ear there are three tiny bones, the *hammer*, the *anvil* and the *stirrup*, which vibrate when the eardrum does. This makes liquid and hairs in the *cochlea*, in the inner ear, move. Messages about the vibrations move along nerves to the brain. The brain tells us what the sound is. The inner ear also helps us keep our balance.

When sound waves enter the ear, the eardrum vibrates. These vibrations are passed through the small bones (*ossicles*) and the fluid in the cochlea. The vibrations are detected by sound receptors in the cochlea, which convert them into electrical impulses that pass through the *auditory nerve* to the brain.

At this stage, the students will be learning that we hear a sound when it enters our ear; they do not need to know about the structure of the ear in any detail. More able students may ask questions about how an ear 'works'; these should be answered at a level the student is able to understand.

Introduction

• Ask the students: *Can you describe how we hear a sound?* (The sound comes from a sound source and travels to our ears.) Accept any reasonable answer but reinforce the idea that a sound from a sound source travels to our ears where we hear it. Remind the students of the words: *sense organ, ear, hear* and *hearing*.

• Bang a ruler on a desk, or make another sound. Ask: *What part of your body did you use to hear the sound?* (ears) Make the noise again and ask the students to raise their hand as soon as they hear the sound. Explain that all humans hear sound in the same way.

• Ask the students to look at Student's Book pages 80–81. Read through the text with the students and make sure they understand that we hear things when a sound enters our ears. Explain that our ears send a message to our brain, which tells us what the sound is. If necessary, listen to Audio clips P1 and P2 again to reinforce the idea that we are able to identify different sources of sound. Answer question 3 as a class, and write the descriptive words on the board for the students to learn. Read each one out loud and ask the students to repeat it, ensuring they use the correct pronunciation.

Teaching and learning activities

- In pairs, ask the students to look at Student's Book page 81 and to answer questions 4 and 5. After a few minutes, come together as a class again and discuss how some sounds can warn us of danger or alert us to a situation. Ask each pair if they can give an example of a sound that helps to keep us safe. (for example, fire alarm, emergency siren, vehicle reversing warning, a person shouting) Ask the students if any of them can describe a situation where hearing a sound has helped to protect them from harm.

- In groups, ask the students to take turns to wear the ear defenders (or to cover their ears with their hands). Have one member of the group tap on a drum or other object trying to make the sound softer (quieter) each time. The student wearing the ear defenders should say when they can no longer hear the sound. Ask: *Why is it more difficult to hear a sound when you are wearing the ear defenders?* (The ear defenders block the sound and prevent it travelling into the ear.) *Can you think of any situations where you would want to block out the sound?* (in a noisy environment, for example a construction site) *Why?* (to protect your ears form loud noises) Elicit that very loud noises can be dangerous and can damage a person's hearing.

- Play a 'whisper race' game with the class. Divide the students into two teams and have them stand in straight lines. Whisper the same message to the students at the head of both lines; when you give the signal they must whisper the message to the person next to them. The message should be passed along the line to the student at the end. When the last student hears the message they should raise their hand. But, the first team to raise their hand may not be the winner! Ask the students to say out loud the message they were given. The winning team is the one that has passed on the message with the lowest number of errors.

Graded activities

1 Give small groups of students a large sheet of paper, old magazines and coloured pens. Ask them to produce a poster to show some sounds

that warn us of danger. Circulate and make suggestions to any groups that need extra help.

2 Give each group of students a selection of different objects and a wooden spoon or drumstick to strike them with. Ask them to write the name of the object and to predict what noise it will make when it is struck with the wooden spoon. The students should use PCM P10 to record their predictions. Let the students strike each object with the spoon, ensuring they do not use excessive force. They should then write the result in their table and whether their prediction was correct. Ask the students to sort the objects into groups based on the sounds that they made. Ask: *Can you make any different groups?*

3 Ask the students to turn to Workbook page 64. They should draw a picture to show how they hear sounds. Remind them that they will need to draw a source of the sound. Help the students to label their drawings. If any students need extra help, tell them to look again at the picture on Student's Book page 80.

Consolidate and review

- In groups, ask the students to create a short role-play to demonstrate how difficult it can be to hear when there is a lot of loud noise. They could role-play people living near an airport or people in the street with emergency vehicles and traffic passing by.

Differentiation

■ All of the students should be able to make a poster to show some sounds that warn us of danger, with little or no help.

● Most of the students should be able to write the name of the object and correctly predict what sound it will make when it is struck. They should be able to sort the objects according to the sounds they make without any help

▲ Some of the students should be able to draw, from memory, an accurate picture that depicts how we hear sounds. They will be able to add clear labels without any help. Most of the students will refer to the Student's Book for guidance when drawing their pictures and may need some help with the labelling.

5.4 Our sense of hearing

Student's Book pages 82–83

Physics learning objectives

- Identify many sources of sound.
- Know that we hear when sound enters our ear.

Resources

- Workbook pages 65, 66 and 67
- PCM P11: Shakers

Classroom equipment

- a selection of pre-prepared shakers
- soft blindfolds
- a selection of objects with which to make different sounds (for example, tambourine, shaker, drum, recorder, glass bottle, newspaper)

Note: For this lesson have ready some pre-prepared shakers. These can easily be made from empty plastic drinks bottles filled with lentils, small stones, etc. Make at least two of each sort and cover with black paper so the students cannot see the contents.

Scientific enquiry skills

- *Ideas and evidence:* Try to answer questions by collecting evidence through observation.
- *Plan investigative work:* Ask questions and contribute to discussions about how to seek answers; make predictions; decide what to do to try to answer a science question.
- *Obtain and present evidence:* Explore and observe in order to collect evidence (measurements and observations) to answer questions; suggest ideas and follow instructions; record stages in work.
- *Consider evidence and approach:* Compare what happened with predictions.

⚠️ Be aware of any students who may have a hearing impairment, and adapt the lesson accordingly.

Scientific background

Living creatures use all of their senses to survive and to learn more about their world. Our ears hear because moving air makes our eardrums and small bones in our ears vibrate, sending electrical signals to our brain.

The human ear is capable of hearing many sounds, but not all of them. Any frequency below the human range is known as *infrasound*. It is so low it can only be heard by creatures with large ears, such as elephants. *Ultrasound* is above the range of the human ear. Bats, whales, and dolphins use ultrasound for navigation.

At this stage, the students will be learning that humans and other animals hear a sound when it enters the ear; they do not need to know about the structure of the ear in any detail. More able students may ask questions about how an ear 'works'; these should be answered at a level the student is able to understand.

Introduction

- Ask the students to look at the pictures of the owl, bat and the dolphin on Student's Book pages 82–83. Explain that it is not just humans that have a good sense of hearing. Some animals depend upon their hearing in order to survive. Ask the students

to discuss questions 1 and 2 in groups. Circulate and listen to what the students are saying. Lead the students to understand that owls and bats are *nocturnal*; they are awake at night when it is dark. They therefore need to be able to hear well so they can find food and stay safe.

- Ask the students: *Are human and animal ears the same?* Accept any reasonable answers, but elicit that animals and humans have two ears. Ask: *Why do we have two ears?* Some of the students may suggest it is easier to hear with two ears. Explain that having two ears helps us (and animals) to detect where the sound has come from. Students do not need to go into further detail at this stage, they should just be aware of the science.

Teaching and learning activities

- Remind the students of the investigation they did in Unit 5.1 where they sat quietly and listened. Say they are going to do this again. Ask the students to sit quietly for one minute and to listen carefully. Ask the students what they heard, and write a list on the board. Next, ask them to sit quietly for another minute, but this time they should close their eyes.

Ask: *Did you hear anything different? Could you hear the clock? People breathing? Footsteps in the corridor? Cars outside?* Add the additional sounds to the list. Ask: *Was it easier to concentrate on the sounds when your eyes were closed? Was it more difficult? Could you tell which direction the sounds were coming from?* Ask the students to close their eyes again; walk around the room and make a sound and ask the students to point to the direction of the sound. Ask: *Can you guess what the source of the sound is? Is it easy to identify a sound when you cannot see the source?*

● Divide the students into four groups, *spring*, *summer*, *autumn* and *winter* telling students to keep the name of their group a secret. Explain that they are going to make some sounds to the rest of the class and they have to guess which season they are. Tell them they should be as creative as possible and use sound sources from nature, such as birds, animals and weather conditions, as well as human-made sounds, for example a lawnmower or an air-conditioning unit.

Graded activities

1 Ask the students to look at the pictures on Workbook page 65. They should match each ear to the animal it belongs to. Circulate, asking questions to guide them as necessary.

2 Give each group a selection of covered shakers (see Notes, above). Ask the students to shake them and to match the shakers that sound the same. They should try and predict what is in the shakers; prompt them by asking questions such as: *Is it one item or many? Are the items large or small? Hard or soft?* Students can use PCM P11 to record their predictions. Let the students unwrap the shakers to see if their predictions were correct.

3 Tell the students they are going to investigate how well they can hear when they are wearing a blindfold. Put the students into groups of mixed ability. Help the students to read through the investigation on Workbook page 66. Then let them make their predictions and draw or write their plan. In pairs, let one student wear a blindfold while the other student uses three or four different objects to produce a sound, standing in a different place each time. The blindfolded student should point to the source of the sound and guess what the source of the sound is. The students should

swap roles and do the investigation again, but this time using a different set of objects (they can swap their objects with another group). Next, ask the students to turn to Workbook page 67, help them to read the instructions and to complete the activity.

Consolidate and review

● Make a list on the board of some animals that have a good sense of hearing. Compare the animals' sense of hearing with that of a human. Ask questions such as: *Can we hear as well as a lion?* There are no right or wrong answers, the object of the exercise is to get the students to think about how well humans can hear and to assess their learning and understanding so far in this topic.

● Ask the students how they detect sounds. Ask: *Are you using your ears at this moment?* Discuss with the class that the sense organ that detects sounds is the ear, and that some sounds are more familiar than others.

Differentiation

■ All of the students should be able to match the ears to the animals without any help.

● Most of the students should be able to match the shakers that sound the same. They can make good guesses as to the material inside the shaker and record their predictions on PCM P11 without any help.

▲ Some of the students should be able to independently write plans and predictions for their investigation in their Workbook. They should be able to work collaboratively and then explain their reasoning. They will be able to concentrate when blindfolded and make accurate guesses as to the source of the sound. More able students may begin to make the connections between loud and soft sounds, and distance. Less able students will find planning the investigation more difficult. Having mixed ability groups should help them to raise their levels of understanding. More able students will be able to say if the investigation was fair or not and offer suggestions for improving it.

5.5 Loud and soft sounds

Student's Book pages 84–85

Physics learning objectives

- Know that we hear when sound enters our ear.
- Recognise that as sound travels from a source it becomes fainter.

Resources

- Workbook pages 68, 69, 70 and 71
- PCM P12: Making a shaker

Classroom equipment

- a selection of different musical instruments
- stopwatch
- materials to make shakers: plastic bottles with lids, funnels, lentils, pasta, small stones, rice, etc. to put into the bottles

Scientific enquiry skills

- *Ideas and evidence:* Try to answer questions by collecting evidence through observation.
- *Plan investigative work:* Ask questions and contribute to discussions about how to seek answers; make predictions; decide what to do to try to answer a science question.
- *Obtain and present evidence:* Explore and observe in order to collect evidence (measurements and observations) to answer questions; suggest ideas and follow instructions; record stages in work.
- *Consider evidence and approach:* Make comparisons; compare what happened with predictions; model and communicate ideas in order to share, explain and develop them.

Key words

- **loud**
- **soft**

⚠️ Be aware of any students who may have a hearing impairment, and adapt the lesson accordingly. If the students use the internet, ensure they do so safely and under adult supervision. Supervise the students when they use scissors.

Scientific background

Sound is the movement of energy through a gas, liquid or solid in longitudinal waves. Sound is produced when energy causes an object to vibrate. The more energy is put in, the louder the sound will be, for example hitting a drum, blowing a whistle.

Our voices act like a musical instrument. Air from our lungs is passed over the vocal cords, which vibrate to make a sound. We need to have enough air in our lungs to sing loudly, or at all. Having more breath allows us to sing for longer or more loudly. Singing loudly pushes more air over the vocal chords, but takes more energy.

At this stage, the students will be learning that we hear a sound when it enters our ear. Some students may start to ask questions about how sound travels to the ear; this should be explained in simple terms as the science will be covered in much greater detail in Stage 4 of this course.

Introduction

- Remind the students of the shaker investigation they did in the previous lesson, Ask them to describe the sounds that the shakers made. Lead them to use the words *loud* and *soft*. Suggest some other words such as *noisy* and *quiet*; write these on the board.

- Let the students explore a selection of musical instruments. Ask them if they can make soft sounds and loud sounds using the same instrument. Ask: *What did you do to make the loud sounds?* Answers will vary depending on the instruments, but you should elicit that they have to be struck, blown or plucked harder (with more force). Repeat, asking: *What did you do to make the soft sounds?*

- Ask: *Is there another way to make the sounds louder or softer?* Suggest that you could move closer to or further away from the source of the sound. Let the students tell the class about their experiences of hearing loud noises but from far away, for example an airplane, a music concert. Some students may struggle with this concept and say that the sound is soft. Accept this as an answer at this stage. Students will learn more about sound in Stage 4 of this course. Ask the students to look at Student's Book pages 84–85 and answer questions 1–5 as a class.

Teaching and learning activities

● Tell the students that they are going to investigate how long they can sing a note. Use a stopwatch to time how long the students can sing for. Now ask them to sing the same note as loudly as they can, and time how long the note lasts. Ask: *Do you think you sang for longer when you were singing louder? Why did you stop singing? Did you run out of breath sooner when you sang louder?* Now time how long the students can sing quietly. Ask them: *Why could you sing for longer when you sang quietly?* Tell the students to breathe out as far as they can, and then try to sing a note as loudly as they can. Ask: *Can you explain why you could not sing?* Tell the students to take a large breath in, and then try to sing a note as loudly as they can. Ask: *What has happened to the volume of your voice?* You could try asking the students to sing a song at different volumes, to see whether singing loudly makes them more tired than singing quietly.

Graded activities

1 Ask the students to look at the pictures on Workbook page 68. Explain that they are going to draw lines from each source of sound to a number. The numbers 1 to 5 represent how loud the sound is, with 5 being the loudest. If necessary, help students by completing the first one as an example. When they have finished, discuss the results. Some children may have ranked the sounds differently to others. Ask individual students to explain to the class why they have put the pictures in a particular order. Encourage them to use words such as *loud, soft, quiet, noisy, low, high, deep*. It might be useful to write some descriptive words on the board for the students to use.

2 Give each student a copy of PCM P12 and the equipment they will need to make a shaker (have a variety of fillings to put inside the shakers so they are not all the same). Go through the instructions on PCM P12 and then let them make their shakers. Circulate and offer guidance to any students that find the task difficult. Ask the students to draw a picture of their finished shaker, and to describe it, on Workbook page 69. Encourage them to use words such as *loud, soft,*

quiet, noisy, etc. to describe the sound that their shaker makes.

3 The students should plan and carry out an investigation using their shakers. Ask them to turn to Workbook page 70. Read through the text with the students and then let them complete the sentences and make their predictions. They can use the descriptive words you have written on the board to help them. Let them test their shakers. They should record the results on Workbook page 71. Ask the students to compare their predictions with their results.

Consolidate and review

● Let the students use their shakers. Ask them to make a loud sound. And then a soft sound. Let them start with a soft sound and get louder.

Differentiation

■ All of the students should be able to draw lines from the sound sources to the numbers. Most will understand the ranking system being used, although less able students will need additional help with this concept. All of the students should be able to use a variety of descriptive words.

● Most of the students should be able to follow the instructions in the correct order and make a shaker. All of the students will be able to draw a picture of their shaker and be able to describe the sound it makes.

▲ Some of the students should be able to independently write plans and predictions for their investigation in their Workbook. They should be able to explain their reasoning. More able students will be able to say if the investigation was fair or not and offer suggestions for improving it.

Big Cat 🐾

Students who have read *Big Cat Pam naps* will be familiar with the idea that sound travels, and will be intrigued by how much noise can go on around Pam before she wakes up.

Students who have read *Big Cat How to make a maraca* may be inspired to make their own musical instruments, to supplement what they have done in the lesson.

5.6 Sound and distance

Student's Book pages 86–87

Physics learning objective

- Recognise that as sound travels from a source it becomes fainter.

Resources

- Workbook pages 72, 73, 74 and 75
- PCM P13: Sound and distance

Classroom equipment

- toy train
- ticking clock
- MP3 player or other portable device to play music
- metre rules or long tape measures
- paper and drawing equipment

Scientific enquiry skills

- *Ideas and evidence:* Try to answer questions by collecting evidence through observation.
- *Plan investigative work:* Ask questions and contribute to discussions about how to seek answers; make predictions; decide what to do to try to answer a science question.
- *Obtain and present evidence:* Explore and observe in order to collect evidence (measurements and observations) to answer questions; suggest ideas and follow instructions; record stages in work.
- *Consider evidence and approach:* Make comparisons; compare what happened with predictions; model and communicate ideas in order to share, explain and develop them.

Key words

- **distance**
- **loud**
- **source**
- **soft**

⚠️ Be aware of any students who may have a hearing impairment, and adapt the lesson accordingly. If you take the students out of the classroom, ensure they are safe when they are in the school grounds.

Scientific background

Sounds are produced by vibrations. Vibrations travel away from a source through the air. To hear a sound, the vibrations have to travel from the source of the sound to our ears.

Sound waves spread out from the source, rather like the ripples spreading out on the surface of a pond. Their effect becomes less the further they spread out. By damping the vibrations, the volume of sounds can be reduced. Soundproofing materials work by damping vibrations.

At this stage, the students will be learning that as sounds travels away from its source it becomes fainter and more difficult to hear; they do not need to understand about vibrations and sound waves. Some students may start to ask questions about how sound travels to the ear; this should be explained in simple terms as the science will be covered in much greater detail in Stage 4 of this course.

Introduction

- Ask the students if they have ever been to a train station or an airport. Ask: *What did the train coming into the station sound like?* (It was quiet when it was far away and became louder as it approached.) Let the students take turns to model the sound of a train approaching and leaving a station using a toy train. Make sure that the students understand that the train is the source of the sound.

Teaching and learning activities

- Arrange the children in three lines, standing facing forward. Show them the ticking clock and ensure that they can all hear it. Bring forward any children who cannot, until they can all hear it. Ask them to sit and to cover their ears. Ask whether they can still hear the clock. Tell them to uncover their ears and explain that you are going to move the clock and that they should sit down when they can no longer hear it. Move away from the children with the clock, until all the children have sat down. Ask them to explain how the sound changes (gets fainter) as the clock moves further away.

- Ask the students to look at Student's Book pages 86–87. Answer the questions as a class, helping less able students as necessary.

Graded activities

1 Tell the students that they are going to investigate what happens to a sound as you move further away from the source. Take the students into the hall or, if it is a fine still day, outside onto the playing field if possible. Line the students up across the hall/field and explain that you are going to play some music. The students will have their backs to you and should walk away until they cannot hear the music any more. When all of the students have stopped, measure the distance that they have walked (this does not have to be an accurate measurement, for example it could be calculated in paces by the teacher). Repeat the experiment with some louder/quieter music and compare the distances travelled. Establish that the further away you are from the source of a sound, the quieter it becomes. Ask: *From what distance could you hear a quiet sound?* Ask the students to think about the way sound is used as a signal. Ask: *Has anyone heard a sound that is used as a signal for something that is about to happen? How many examples can we think of?* Examples could include emergency service vehicles, flood warning sirens, the fire alarm in school, etc. Back in the classroom you could ask the students to draw a picture to demonstrate how sound is used to warn us of danger.

2 Ask the students to turn to Workbook pages 72–73. Say that they are going to plan their own investigation to see what happens to a sound as you move further away from the source. Read through the text and make sure the students understand what they are going to do. Let them complete their plan and make their predictions. Go though the plans with the students and make sure they are practicable (do not correct any unfair tests, as these can be used as examples with the class).

3 Let the students carry out their investigations. They should record their results on Workbook page 74. Back in the classroom they should compare their predictions with their results, and explain their findings on Workbook page 75. Ask: *Which group had the best plan? Why? Was their investigation a fair test? Why? Why not? What would you change?*

Consolidate and review

● Ask the students to imagine they are somewhere where there is a very loud noise, for example at the launch of a space rocket. Ask: *What can you do to protect your hearing?* (move further away from the source of the sound, wear ear defenders)

● Give each student a copy of PCM P13 and ask them to complete the activity in order to assess their understanding of sound and distance. This is not as straightforward as it first appears. The students' answers will open up opportunities for further discussion.

Differentiation

■ All of the students should be able to take part in the investigation with little or no help. Most will understand that the sound becomes softer/fainter the further away they walk from the source. They will all be able to take part in the class discussion about sounds being used as warnings, drawing examples from personal experience or their knowledge of the wider world.

● Most of the students should be able to independently plan an investigation and make predictions in their Workbook, although some will require additional help to read the text. A few students will find this task difficult and will benefit from more structured guidance from the teacher.

▲ Some of the students should be able to carry out their investigations without any help. They will independently record their results in their Workbook and compare their prediction with the outcome. More able students will be able to say if they think the investigations are fair or not and offer suggestions for improving them.

Big Cat 🐾

Students who have read *Big Cat The pied piper of Hamelin* may wonder how all of the rats – and then the children – heard the piper playing. In this unit they learn more about how sound travels.

Consolidation

Student's Book page 88

Physics learning objectives

• Identify many sources of sound.

• Know that we hear when sound enters our ear.

• Recognise that as sound travels from a source it becomes fainter.

Resources

• Workbook page 76

• Assessment Sheets P3 and P4

Looking back

● Use the summary points on Student's Book page 88 to review the key things that the students have learned in the topic. Ask questions such as: *What can you remember about natural and human-made sounds? Name some. What do we use to hear sounds?* (our ears) *What happens to a sound the closer you are to the source?* (It gets louder.) *What happens to a sound the further away you get from the source?* (It gets fainter/softer.)

● Ask the students to complete the activity on Workbook page 76. They should make a list of some different sounds they can hear at home and write the names in the correct rooms on the picture. Circulate, asking: *What sounds can you hear when you are in the garden/outside? If you are in the bathroom, can you hear the sounds coming from the living room? How many loud/soft sounds can you hear? Can you hear any sounds from natural sources?* This activity will show you how well the students have understood the topic.

How well do you remember?

You may use the revision and consolidation activities on Student's Book page 88, either as a test or as a paired class activity. If you are using the activities as a test, have the students work on their own to complete the tasks in writing, and then collect and mark the work. If you are using them as a class activity, you may prefer to let the students do the tasks orally. Circulate as they discuss the questions and observe the students carefully to see who is confident and who is unsure of the concepts.

For question 1, play some audio clips of different animals for the students to identify.

Some suggested answers

1 Answers will depend on the audio clips.

2 Picture A: TV, computer, cat, people, fire, etc. Picture B: radio, etc.

3 Students' own answers.

Assessment

A more formal assessment of the students' understanding of the topic can be undertaken using Assessment Sheets P3 and P4. These can be completed in class or as a homework task.

Students following Cambridge Primary Science Framework will write progression tests set and supplied by Cambridge Assessment International Education at this level and feedback will be given regarding their achievement levels.

Assessment Sheet answers

Sheet P3

1 bird, drum [2]

2 Students' own drawings. [3]

3 ear [1]

4 Students' own answers. [2]

5 Students' own answers. [2]

Sheet P4

1 trumpet - blow, guitar - pluck, drum - strike [3]

2 soft, softly [2]

3 move further away from the source, wear ear defenders [2]

4 fire alarm, police siren [2]

5 True [1]

Student's Book answers

Pages 76–77

1 Answers might include: talking, shouting, footsteps, etc.
2 Answers might include: traffic, people talking, a road drill, baby crying, ambulance siren, etc.
3 Answers might include: windows, clothes, etc.
4 Answers might include: shouting, banging, engine noises, etc.
5 Answers might include: the man is shouting, the digger is moving, the digger's engine is working, etc.

Pages 78–79

1 Guitar, whistle, bell, phone, alarm clock, drum.
2 It rings when you shake it. / It vibrates and makes a sound.
3 Blow it. / Push air into it.
4 They are making sounds/music using musical instruments (and they are singing).
5 They are moving/shaking/striking/hitting/tapping the instruments.

Pages 80–81

1 Ears.
2 Sense of hearing.
3 The cat might purr or miaow. The fizzy water might fizz. The steel drum will make a ringing sound.
4 Fire engine – warns us to get out of the way; baby crying – alerts us that it needs something/has hurt itself/is hungry/tired.
5 Answers might include: someone shouting a warning, a flood or other weather warning, a police siren, a vehicle reversing warning.

Pages 82–83

1 It helps the owl to hear small sounds in the dark so it can locate its food. It keep the owl safe from danger.
2 So it can listen for small insects (prey) in the dark.
3 Students' own answers.
4 Students' own answers.
5 It is more difficult to identify a sound source when you cannot see it.

Pages 84–85

1 Environment B.
2 Environment A.
3 Environment A: traffic, people talking, people walking, a road drill, headphones, etc. Environment B: birds singing, wind blowing, etc.
4 Loud sounds: lightning, fireworks, digger. Soft sounds: water, mouse, snake.
5 Loud sound: strike it with more force/harder. Soft sound: strike it with less force/gently.

Pages 86–87

1 The child at the front of the line and the boys wearing headphones.
2 The boy at the front is further away from the source of the sound. The two boys who are wearing headphones cannot hear the drum.
3 Answers might include: birds singing, airplane, wind, footsteps, talking, singing, etc.

PCM B1: Living or non-living?

Cut out the pictures and sort them into living and non-living things.
Colour them in and use them to make a poster.

PCM B2: **Plants or animals? (1)**

Cut out the pictures and sort them into plants and animals.

PCM B2: Plants or animals? (2)

PCM B3: Elham and the beans (1)

One day, Elham was walking home from school when she saw an old man trying to cross the road.

'Would you like me to help you?' she asked kindly.

The old man smiled and nodded, and Elham helped him across the busy road.

'You must let me repay your kindness, little girl. I don't have much, but here, have these beans. I tried to sell them at the market, but everyone said they were too old and shrivelled,' said the man.

Elham took the beans and thanked the old man, and went on her way.

When she got home, she showed her mother the beans and told her how she had come by them.

'Those beans are too old and shrivelled for me to cook, Elham. Go and put them in the bin,' said her mother.

Elham looked sadly at her beans and decided to ask her father if she could plant them.

She found her father in the garden. She showed him the beans and told him how she had come by them.

'Those beans are too old and shrivelled to plant, Elham. Go and put them in the bin,' said her father.

Elham looked sadly at her beans and was just about to put them in the bin when her grandfather called her.

'What do you have there, little Elham?' asked Grandfather.

Elham showed him her beans and told him the story of how she had come by them.

'Your mother is right, they are too old too cook. But they might grow,' he said kindly. He found a little pot for her and showed her how to plant the beans. 'Make sure you water them and maybe they will grow,' he said.

Elham watered her little pot every day, not too much but just enough. Every day her father would tell her, 'Those beans were too old, they will not grow,' and every day Elham would smile and reply, 'They might, Father.'

PCM B3: Elham and the beans (2)

Every night Elham would make sure the pot was safe on the window sill, and every night her mother would say, 'Those beans were too old, they will not grow,' and every night Elham would smile and reply, 'They might, Mother.'

One day, when Elham went to check the little pot, she saw tiny little green leaves peeping through the soil.

The next day, her bean plants were as tall as her fingers.

The next day, they were as tall as her hand.

Elham's grandfather helped her to plant the bean plants in the garden, and every day Elham would water them and every day the plants grew taller.

'Those beans were too old, they will not flower,' said her father. Elham smiled and said, 'They might, Father.'

Soon her bean stalks were so tall she couldn't see the tops of them, and they were covered in delicate little red flowers.

'Those beans were too old, they will not produce pods,' said her mother. Elham smiled and said, 'They might, Mother.'

Soon the flowers fell from the bean plants, but in their place Elham found tiny pods starting to form.

'Those beans were too old, the pods will not swell,' said her father. Elham smiled and said, 'They might, Father.'

Over the next few days, Elham and her grandfather watched as the pods grew in length and swelled. Soon the plants were covered in the longest, greenest, fattest beans they had ever seen.

The next day Grandfather told Elham the beans were ready to be picked. She helped him collect a basket full of the biggest, greenest beans and she took them to her mother.

'Those beans were too old, the pods will be dry and tasteless,' said her mother. Elham smiled and said, 'They might not be, Mother.'

Mother smiled and cooked the beans for their dinner. They were the best beans everyone had ever tasted. Elham's father even asked for seconds.

PCM B4: **Will it grow?**

Draw a picture of each pot.

Pot with cress seeds

Pot with stones

PCM B5: **Five little leaves**

Five green leaves, hanging on a tree,
Enjoying the sun, and swinging free,
Along came the wind, blowing past the shore,
Blew away a leaf, and then there were four.

Four green leaves, hanging on a tree,
Enjoying the sun, and swinging free,
Along came the wind, blowing from the sea,
Blew away a leaf, and then there were three.

Three green leaves, hanging on a tree,
Enjoying the sun, and swinging free,
Along came the wind, blowing through the bamboo,
Blew away a leaf, and then there were two.

Two green leaves, hanging on a tree,
Enjoying the sun, and swinging free,
Along came the wind, blowing from the sun,
Blew away a leaf, and then there was one.

One green leaf, hanging on a tree,
Enjoying the sun, and swinging free,
Along came the wind, its blowing almost done,
Blew away a leaf, and then there were none.

PCM B6: **Plants I can see**

Do you have any plants at home? Draw them here.

Did you see plants on your walk to school?

Draw them here. Say where they were.

PCM B7: **Comparing seeds**

Collect some seeds from different fruits.

Use sticky tape to stick them here.

Which fruit were they from? Write the names under the seeds.

In what ways are they the same?

In what ways are they different?

Things that are the same	Things that are different

PCM B8: **Plant heads**

You will need:
- a clean, small yoghurt pot
- cotton wool
- mustard or garden cress seeds
- kitchen towel
- water
- paint and brush

Instructions

1 Paint a funny face on your yoghurt pot and write your name on the back.

2 Put some wet kitchen towel into the bottom of your pot.

3 Put some damp cotton wool on top of the kitchen towel.

4 Sprinkle some seeds over the cotton wool.

5 Put your pot on the window ledge.

6 Remember to keep the cotton wool damp.

7 Wait for your plant head to grow!

PCM B9: **Lemon tree life cycle (1)**

Cut out the stages of the lemon tree life cycle.

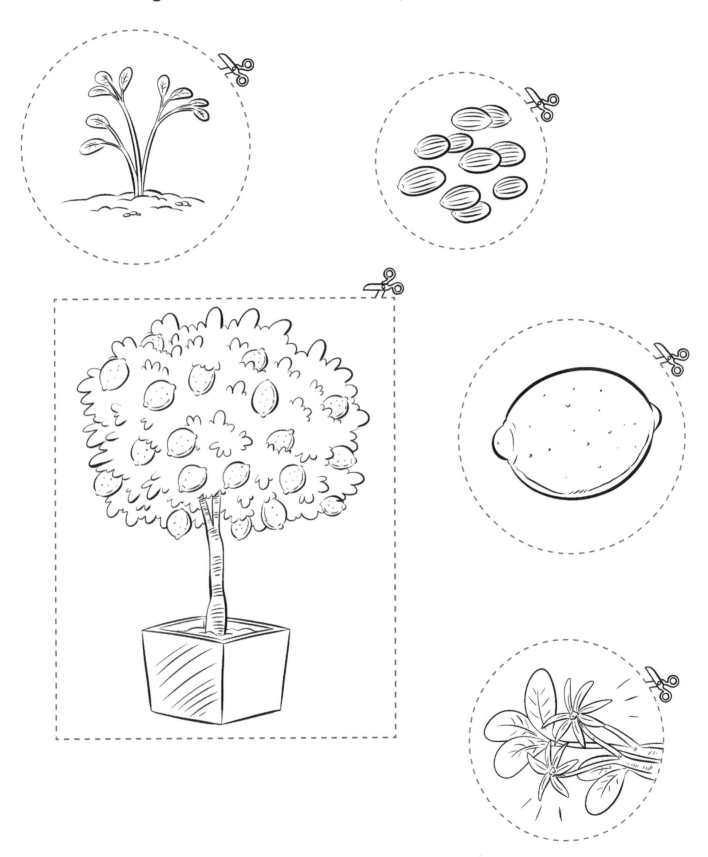

PCM B10: Lemon tree life cycle (2)

Glue them in the correct order.

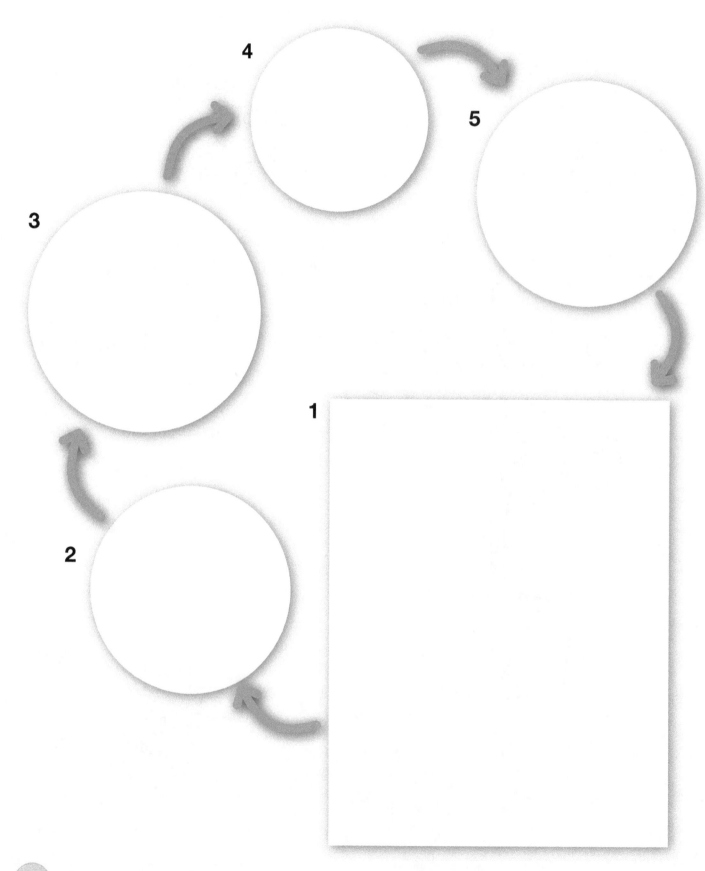

PCM B11: **My family**

Draw pictures of your family in the boxes below.

In what ways are their faces and their bodies similar to yours?

This is _____	This is _____
This is _____	This is _____

PCM B12: **Picture of my friend**

Draw a picture of your friend in this box.

This is a picture of _____

I can tell who it is because of their

hair colour _____

hair style _____

eye colour _____

face shape _____

PCM B13: **Spot the differences**

There are five differences to find. Draw a circle around each difference.

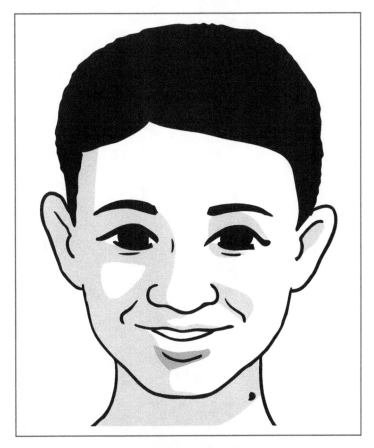

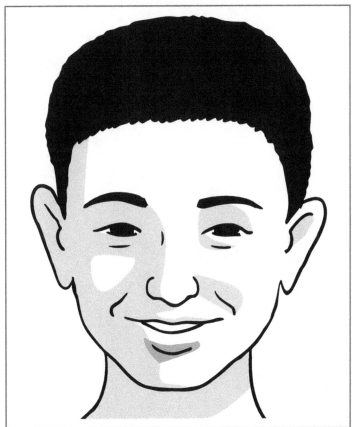

PCM B14: **Where do you wear it?**

Look at the pictures. Draw a line from each piece of clothing to the body part that you wear it on.

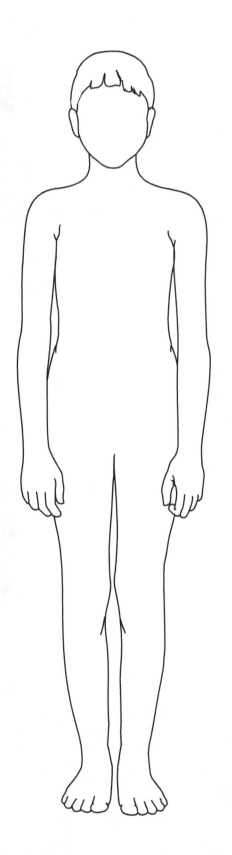

PCM B15: Food match

Picture cards

✂

Word cards

✂

donut	pizza	cheese	cereal	salad
banana	chocolate slice	orange	orange juice	mushroom
raspberries	grapes	chicken leg	tomato	milk
cake	pineapple	pear	apple	lettuce
bread	yoghurt	lemon	strawberry	chocolate

PCM B16: School menu

Design a healthy menu for a week at your school.

Write or draw what you would like to eat each day.

Monday	
Tuesday	
Wednesday	
Thursday	
Friday	

Which is your favourite meal? _____

PCM B17: **Spot the differences**

There are five differences to find. Draw a circle around each difference.

PCM B18: Wasting water

Draw a circle around each place where water is being wasted.

PCM B19: Filtering water

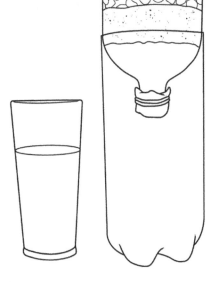

What you will need

- 2-litre plastic bottle
- scissors
- cotton fabric
- elastic band
- cotton wool
- washed sand
- washed gravel
- water mixed with soil so it looks muddy

Introduction

Water from most sources must be cleaned before it is used because it contains impurities, bacteria and other micro-organisms that can make you ill.

This experiment demonstrates a simplified version of filtration.

Method

Cut off the top third of a plastic bottle (keep the remaining part).

Use an elastic band to secure a piece of cotton material over the spout of the bottle. Turn it upside down and place it inside the bottom part of the bottle.

Add a layer of cotton wool to the bottom, followed by a layer of sand and then a layer of gravel.

Pour a glass of dirty water (water mixed with soil) through the filter.

Observations

The water looks much clearer once it has passed through the filter.

Explanation

The gravel filters the solid large particles that are not dissolved in the dirty water. The size of the particles that can be removed by filtration depends on the size of the filter you use. The gaps between the grains of sand are smaller than those between the pieces of gravel, so sand will stop more dirt particles from getting through than the gravel will. The cotton wool, and finally the cotton fabric, should remove even more.

Safety

The water must not be drunk even after filtering, as it may still contain bacteria from the soil.

PCM B20: **Fruity smells**

Smell each pot and draw a picture of the fruit that you think is inside it.

1	2
3	4

PCM B21: Senses in action

What senses are the people in the picture using?

Person	Which senses are they using?	Why?

PCM C1: **Describing materials**

hard	soft	shiny
dull	bendy	smooth
rough	see-through	flexible
warm	cold	strong

PCM C2: Cardboard glasses

Copy on to card and cut out.

PCM C3: **Concrete or glass?**

List some objects made from concrete or glass that you might see on a tour of your school grounds.

Put a tick (✓) if you see them. Put a cross (✗) if you do not see them.

Objects made from concrete	Seen on tour?	Objects made from glass	Seen on tour?

PCM C4: **Sorting materials**

Sort the pictures into fabric, metal, wood and stone.

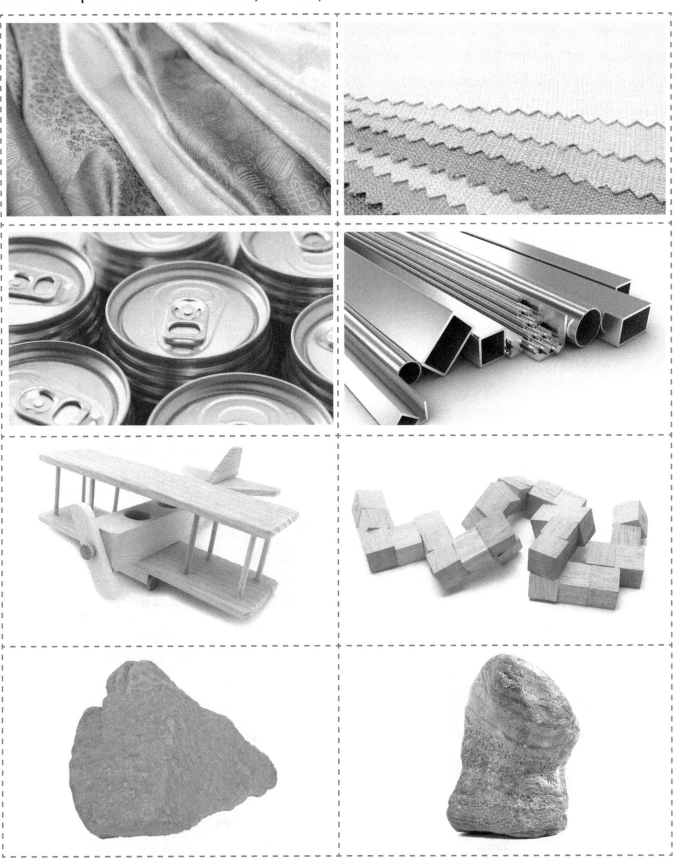

PCM P1: Animal movement

PCM P2: **Pushing and pulling**

Draw toys that work by pushing and toys that work by pulling.

Toys that work by pushing	Toys that work by pulling

PCM P3: Making a waterwheel

What you will need

- stiff cardboard
- a plate to draw round
- scissors and sticky tape
- skewer

1 Cut two large, matching circles from the cardboard.

2 Cut a long strip of card, and then cut this into smaller, equally-sized, rectangular pieces.

3 Take one circle of card and tape the rectangular pieces evenly around the edges.

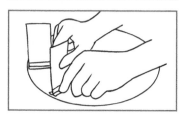

4 Now tape on the other cardboard circle.

5 Put a skewer through the middle of the wheel, as shown.

6 Hold both ends of the skewer.

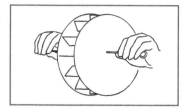

7 Hold the waterwheel under a gently running tap and watch it turn.

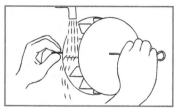

PCM P4: **How far does it travel?**

Roll a ball gently, using a small force. Then roll the ball more strongly, using a big force.

Draw pictures to show what happened.

This is what happened when I _____ the ball gently.

This is what happened when I _____ the ball more strongly.

PCM P5: **Toy bumping**

Roll two toy cars towards each other. Write what you did. Remember to use the words 'push' and 'force'.

This is what I did: _____

_____

_____

Now draw a picture to show what happened.

PCM P6: **Sound source survey**

Write or draw a picture of each sound you hear and its source.

Sound	Source
whistling	a bird in the tree

PCM P7: **Musical instruments**

Draw a line to show how to play each instrument.

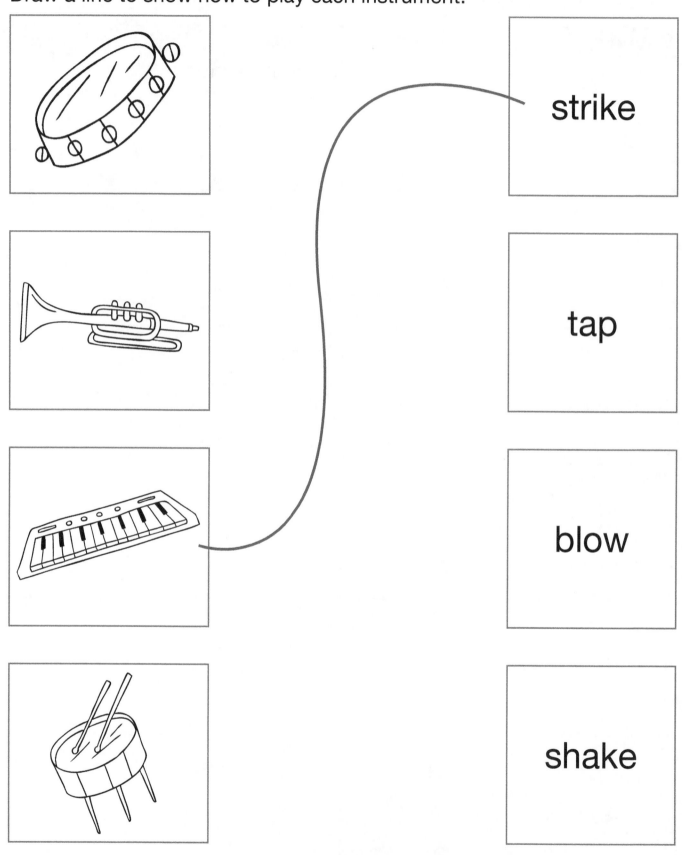

PCM P8: **Sound word cards**

strike	pluck
blow	shake

PCM P9: **Blow, pluck or strike?**

Draw an instrument in each circle that is played like this.

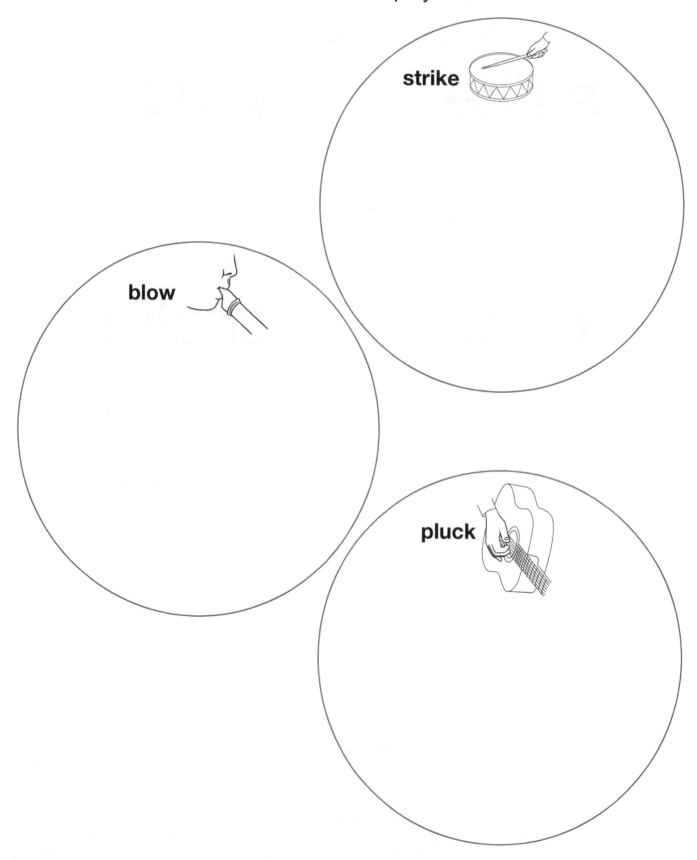

PCM P10: **Different sounds**

Predict what sound the different objects will make when you strike them.

Object	I predict it will make a _____ sound	What sound it actually made	Was my prediction correct?
glass bottle	ringing	ringing	yes

PCM P11: Shakers

Predict what is inside the shaker.

	What I predict is inside the shaker	What is actually inside	Was my prediction correct?
Shaker 1			
Shaker 2			
Shaker 3			
Shaker 4			
Shaker 5			

PCM P12: Making a shaker

What you will need
- empty plastic bottle with a lid
- items to put inside the bottle
- funnel

1

2

3

4

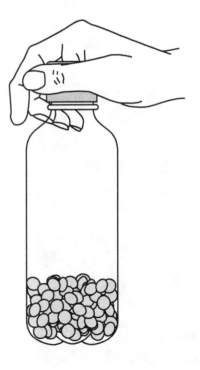

PCM P13: Sound and distance

Investigate how far away you will be able to hear each sound.
Tick (✓) the correct answers.

Sound	Close by	A short distance away	A long distance away	Very far away

Biology: **Assessment Sheet B1**

1 Draw three living things.

[3 marks]

2 Draw three non-living things.

[3 marks]

3 What can living things do? Tick (✓) the correct answers.

move ☐   live without water ☐   grow ☐   [2 marks]

4 True or false? Circle the correct answer.

Seeds grow into plants.   True   False   [1 mark]

5 Name one thing that has never been alive.

_____   [1 mark]

[Total: _____ /10]

Biology: **Assessment Sheet B2**

1 Label the picture of the plant.
Use the words in the box
to help you.

fruit stem flower leaf root

[5 marks]

2 Which of these animals live in a cold environment? Draw a line from each animal to the word.

cold

Which environment does the camel live in? Circle the correct answer.

rainforest   desert   ocean   [4 marks]

3 True or false? Circle the correct answer.

Fish live in water.   True   False   [1 mark]

[Total: _____ /10]

Biology: **Assessment Sheet B3**

1 Put the plant life cycle in the correct order. Draw a line to join each number to the correct stage. The first one has been done for you.

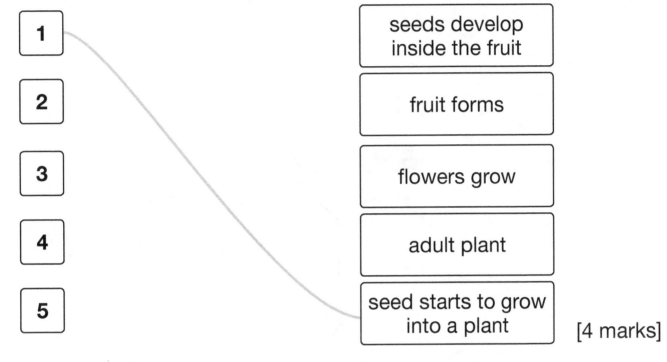

1		seeds develop inside the fruit
2		fruit forms
3		flowers grow
4		adult plant
5		seed starts to grow into a plant

[4 marks]

2 Which two roots can we eat? Circle the correct answers.

tomato   **sweet potato**   **tree**   **carrot**   **sunflower**   [2 marks]

3 Which animal is the odd one out? Tick the correct box.

Why is it the odd one out? _____   [2 marks]

4 True or false? Circle the correct answers.

All animals need to eat food and drink water. True False

A wooden chair is a living thing.   True False   [2 marks]

[Total: _____ /10]

Biology: Assessment Sheet B4

1 Label the parts of the body. Use the words in the box to help you.

| head   finger   foot   arm   chest   hand   neck   leg | [8 marks] |

2 Name two features that all animals have.

_____ [2 marks]

[Total: _____ /10]

Biology: **Assessment Sheet B5**

1 Name two things we should eat less of to stay healthy.

_____ [2 marks]

2 Name two things we should eat more of to stay healthy.

_____ [2 marks]

3 Circle the odd one out.

Why is it the odd one out?

_____ [2 marks]

4 Circle the correct word in each sentence.

The place that water comes from is called a **source** / **house**.

Seawater has **salt** / **sugar** in it and is not good to drink.   [2 marks]

5 True or false? Circle the correct answers.

We should eat a healthy diet.   True   False

Dirty water is safe to drink.   True   False   [2 marks]

[Total: _____ /10]

Biology: **Assessment Sheet B6**

1 Look at the picture of the boy. Draw a line from each sense word to the correct sense organ.

sight

smell

touch

hearing

[4 marks]

2 Look at the pictures of the boys.

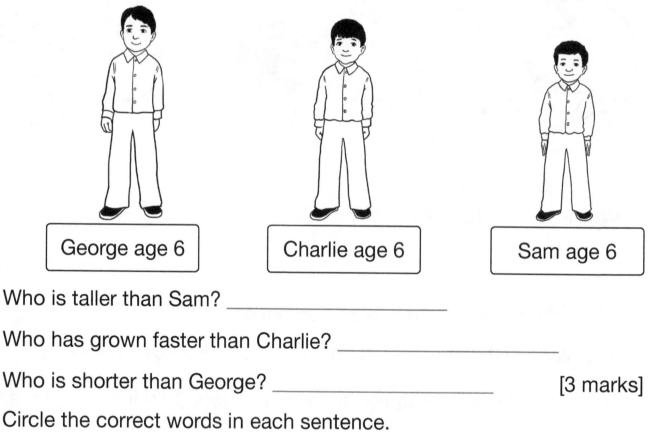

George age 6

Charlie age 6

Sam age 6

Who is taller than Sam? _____

Who has grown faster than Charlie? _____

Who is shorter than George? _____

[3 marks]

3 Circle the correct words in each sentence.

When you cross the road, you should **look** / **smell** and **touch** / **listen** to stay safe.

Our senses keep us **safe** / **sad**.

[3 marks]

[Total: _____ /10]

Chemistry: **Assessment Sheet C1**

1 Name something that can be made from each material. Use a word from the box to describe one property of the material.

Material	What can be made from it?	Property of the material
plastic		
stone		
wood		
glass		
paper		

shiny	heavy	strong	smooth	hard
light	rough	flexible		see-through
soft	dull	waterproof		absorbent

[10 marks]

[Total: _____ /10]

Chemistry: **Assessment Sheet C2**

1 Name two hard materials.

_____ [2 marks]

2 Name two soft materials.

_____ [2 marks]

3 Circle the absorbent materials.

[2 marks]

4 Tick (✓) three properties of glass.

see-through ☐

smooth ☐

rare ☐

easy to clean ☐

absorbent ☐   [3 marks]

5 True or false? Circle the correct answer.

Concrete buildings are very strong.   True   False   [1 mark]

[Total: _____ /10]

Physics: **Assessment Sheet P1**

1 Draw a line from each animal to the way it moves.

swims

walks

flies

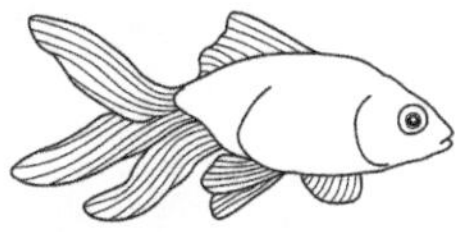

slithers

[4 marks]

2 Circle each picture that shows a pull.

[2 marks]

3 Circle the correct word in each sentence.

A sailing boat moves when the wind **pushes** / **pulls** its sail.

A force on a moving object can make it change **direction** / **colour**.

[2 marks]

4 Complete the sentence using words from the box.

Water is used to turn a waterwheel. Water can _____ with

a very strong _____.

| push | pull | force | sound |

[2 marks]

[Total: _____ /10]

Physics: Assessment Sheet P2

1 Circle the toy that moves by pulling.

[1 mark]

2 Three toy cars were pushed along a track.

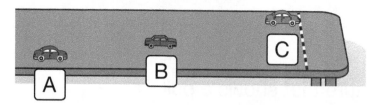

Which car, A, B or C, was given the biggest push? ____

Which car was given the smallest push? ____

Would a toy car move if it was not pushed? ____ [3 marks]

3 True or false? Circle the correct answer.

Heavy objects are easy to push and pull.   True   False

Living things do not move.   True   False   [2 marks]

4 Name two parts of your body that move when you are playing football.

_____ [2 marks]

5 Tick (✓) the correct boxes. When a moving ball hits another object it can:

change direction [ ]

change colour [ ]

slow down [ ]   [2 marks]

[Total: _____ /10]

Physics: **Assessment Sheet P3**

1 Tick (✓) the things that are sources of sound.

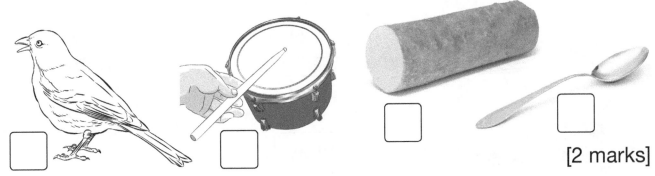

[2 marks]

2 Draw three sources of sounds that you can hear in classroom.

[3 marks]

3 Which sense organ do we use to hear with? Circle the correct answer.

ear   **eye**   **nose**   **mouth**   [1 mark]

4 Name two natural sources of sound.

_____ [2 marks]

5 Name two human-made sources of sound.

_____ [2 marks]

[Total: _____ /10]

Physics: Assessment Sheet P4

1 Draw a line to match each instrument to the way it is played.

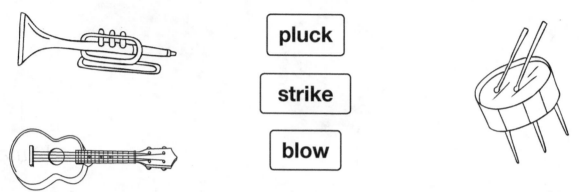

| pluck |
| strike |
| blow |

[3 marks]

2 Circle the correct word in each sentence.

The sound from a source that is far away is **soft / loud**.

To make a trumpet sound quiet, I must blow it very **hard / softly**.

[2 marks]

3 What two things can you do to protect your hearing from loud sounds? Tick the boxes.

move further away from the source ☐

close your eyes ☐

wear ear defenders ☐

[2 marks]

4 Which of these are warning sounds? Circle them.

a fire alarm   a police siren

a cat purring   a telephone ringing

[2 marks]

5 True or false? Circle the correct answer.

The wind is a natural source of sound.   True   False   [1 mark]

[Total: _____ /10]